LETTERS FROM A
BALLET-MASTER

LETTERS FROM A BALLET-MASTER

The Correspondence of Arthur Saint-Léon

Edited by Ivor Guest

Dance Horizons
New York 1981

This edition first published in 1981 by
arrangement with Dance Books Ltd., London

Dance Horizons, 1801 East 26th Street,
Brooklyn, N.Y. 11229

ISBN 0–87127–123–0

Library of Congress Catalog card number 81–65108

Printed in Great Britain

CONTENTS

ILLUSTRATIONS

Between pages 30 and 31

Saint-Léon, the dancer-violinist, in *Le Violon du Diable* (1849), with his wife Fanny Cerrito. *(Bibl. de l'Opéra)*

Saint-Léon, the virtuoso dancer, in *Pâquerette* (1851). Caricature by Marcelin, from the *Journal pour rire* of 14th February 1851.

A page from Saint-Léon's *La Sténochorégraphie*, showing part of the coda of the *pas de six* from *La Vivandière* (1848) recorded in his system of dance notation.

Saint-Léon in 1863. Photograph by Bergamasco of St. Petersburg. *(Collection of Ivor Guest)*

Between pages 62 and 63

Emile Perrin, Director of the Paris Opéra from 1862 to 1870. *(Bibl. de l'Opéra)*

Charles Nuitter, Archivist of the Paris Opéra from 1866 to 1899. *(Bibl. de l'Opéra)*

Marfa Muravieva in *Néméa* (1864). Photograph by Disdéri. *(Bibl. de l'Opéra)*

Saint-Léon rehearsing *Néméa* (1864). From *La Vie Parisienne* of 16th July 1864. *(Bibl. de l'Opéra)*

Between pages 78 and 79

Saint-Léon in rehearsal. Anonymous caricature. *(Archives Nationales)*

Ludwig Minkus. Photograph by B. Braquehais. *(Bibl. Nationale)*

Madame Dominique in 1864. Photograph by S. Bureau. *(Collection of Ivor Guest)*

A page from Saint-Léon's *répétiteur* score of *Il Basilico* (1865) "with scenistenochoreographic details." *(Bibl. de l'Opéra)*

Between pages 94 and 95

Guglielmina Salvioni. *(Collection of Ivor Guest)*

Saint-Léon's instructions for the lances used in *La Source*. See Letter 38. *(Archives Nationales)*

Praskovia Lebedeva. Photograph by Levitsky. *(Bibl. Nationale)*

Adèle Grantzow. Portrait by Léon Flameng. *(Bibl. de l'Opéra)*

Between pages 126 and 127

Léo Delibes. *(Bibl. de l'Opéra)*

Saint-Léon towards the end of his life. Photograph by B. Braquehais. *(Bibl. de l'Opéra)*

Invitation to the funeral of Saint-Léon, sent on behalf of Fanny Cerrito.

Saint-Léon's tomb in the Cemetery of Montmartre. Sculpture by Belmondo (?). Photograph by Jean-Louis Tamvaco.

INTRODUCTION

Ballet is an art without words, and the few letters which have survived from ballet-masters and dancers of the past might suggest that the pen is inimical to the practitioners of an art that expresses itself essentially through movement. There are, of course, exceptions to such a sweeping assertion – August Bournonville and Marie Taglioni spring immediately to mind – but it is nonetheless rare to find prolific and articulate correspondents among the dancing profession.

So it was an exciting discovery – made many years ago in the course of my research into the ballet of the Second Empire – to unearth in the Archives Nationales in Paris a series of letters written by Arthur Saint-Léon to his friend and scenarist, Charles Nuitter. When I re-read them recently after an interval of more than twenty years, I saw them in a wider perspective and recognised the valuable light they shed not only on the personality and the creative pattern of an important choreographer but on the ballet worlds of France and Russia which Saint-Léon dominated in the last few years of his life. His correspondence with Nuitter between 1866 and 1870 forms the greater part of this collection, but through the generosity of private collectors and other institutions I have been able to expand the collection to a total of sixty-four letters and telegrams which cover the greater part of his career.

We owe the preservation of his letters to Nuitter to the latter's recognition of their historical value. Happily for us Charles Nuitter, by the very nature of his vocation as archivist of the Paris Opéra, was an inveterate hoarder of notes and source material from which many generations of scholars of musical and theatrical history have benefited. Saint-Léon's letters were carefully placed by him in the files of the Opéra, where they remain to this day, sometimes complete with the envelope in which they made their journey across Europe to Nuitter's desk. The other side of the correspondence, Nuitter's letters to Saint-Léon, do not appear to have survived, but Saint-Léon's letters themselves, dashed off with such facility that the pen seems to keep up with the writer's thoughts and we seem almost to be hearing him speak, give a rare insight into the man and the artist and reveal, through their warmth, the very close friendship that bound the two men.

★   ★   ★

Saint-Léon was born in Paris on 17th September 1821, and since there has been some confusion about this fact it may be appropriate to quote his birth certificate in full:

> 19th September 1821, midday. Before us, Frédéric Pierre Baron Lecordier, mayor of the first arrondissement of Paris, Officer of the Legion, Chevalier of the Order of St. Michael, there appeared Sieur *Léon Michel*, artist of the Académie Royale de Musique, aged 44 years, residing at 21 rue St. Marc, who produced to us a child of the male sex whom he declared had been born at No. 11 Allée des Veuves on the 17th instant at 3 o'clock in the afternoon, to him and to Dame *Adèle Joséphine Nicolau*, his wife, residing as above, to which child he has given the forenames of *Charles Victor Arthur*.

The child was baptised in the Reformed Church of Paris

on 24th October 1821, his godparents being his mother's sister Victoire and her husband, Jacob Gard.[1]

Nothing is known of his mother. She may have died when he was a child, for in one of his letters to Nuitter (Letter 44) he mentions a Madame Aglaé Gillet as "the lady who brought me up."

His father, Léon Michel, would have been born about 1777. Although he achieved only a modest position at the Paris Opéra, his qualities were recognised by the all-powerful ballet-master, Pierre Gardel. In a report made in 1807 on improving the standard of the "individual combats", Gardel recommended the appointment of "a man who is versed in these exercises, and a musician as well" to assist choreographers in arranging such scenes, and went on to add: "We have in the ballet company a *figurant* called Michel who has all the qualities required to fill this post well. He is first, one of the strongest men in Paris, secondly, an excellent musician, thirdly, a dancer whose positions combine grace with feeling and nobility, and fourthly, is charming and honest."[2] As a result Michel was offered 300 fr. to take charge of a small group of men for the combats, but he refused, although he later changed his mind and applied to be appointed maître d'escrime.

On 1st January 1817 Michel was granted a pension of 329.50 fr.[3] and the Opéra released him from his duties so that he could take up a four-year appointment as Court dancing master in Tuscany. Shortly after his son was born he accepted a similar post at the Court of Württemburg, where for some fourteen years he was dancing master to the princesses.

During his years in Stuttgart Michel-Saint-Léon, as he called himself, wrote down a series of exercises and variations in three notebooks which are now in the Bibliothèque de l'Opéra. One of these, entitled *Cahier*

[1] Archives Nationales, AJ[13] 499
[2] Archives Nationales, AJ[13] 84
[3] Archives Nationales, AJ[13] 176

d'Exercises pour LL. AA. Royales les Princesses de Wurtem-burg 1830, contains a number of dances, including gavottes, a minuet, and significantly in the light of his son's predilection for character dances, boleros, a "kracovia" and a "kosaque". The other two books are entitled *Exercises de 1829* and *2me Cahier Exercises de 1830*. The first contains an "*entrée* composed by Arthur", the second a "variation by Arthur" – the first evidence we have of the precocious talent that was developing.

But this reveals only half the picture, for the boy was a double prodigy, being no less proficient on the violin than he was in his dancing shoes. Indeed it was as a violinist that he first faced an audience, at the König-licher Redouten-Saal in Stuttgart on 16th December 1834, when he performed the solo part in one of Jacques Rode's violin concertos. The programme announced him as a pupil of the Herrn. Barnbeck, but in later years he must have studied under other teachers, and it is possible, if we are to believe a short biography pub-lished in Paris in 1850, that he took lessons from Josef Mayseder and the celebrated Nicolo Paganini.

Although his talents were to be directed primarily to the dance he continued to make occasional appearances as a violinist. As a boy he gave concerts in Munich in 1835 and in Paris in 1837, his repertory including variations by the Czech virtuoso Kalliwoda and Franz Pecháček the younger. His later concerts frequently included compositions of his own, and among his papers preserved at the Archives Nationales is a long list of his works bearing the wry comment "molto favoro ma poco denaro." From this and from programmes of his concerts the list of his musical compositions given in Appendix II has been compiled. Some pieces which he composed in St. Petersburg in the 1860s were adapted for the "sourdine-orgue" or the "sourdine-viole", an invention of his which seems to have been some sort of mute that produced on the violin a tone resembling the organ stop known as the sourdine viole.

10

To obtain an impression of Saint-Léon as violinist we have to rely on contemporary accounts which unfortunately are all too few because his concerts were generally not occasions which the music critics troubled to record. There is, however, a review of his benefit performance during his first season in London, describing how he came rather nervously on to the stage, dressed in a black suit, to play a violin solo of his own composition. The critic of *The Times* reported that his playing was notable for a number of startling "tricks", and gave as examples his "striking pizzicato note at the moment he was bowing, introducing staccatoed harmonic notes and pizzicato notes in quick alternation, [and] jumping skilfully from the fourth to the first string."[4]

The most interesting account of his playing was written by Adolphe Adam, composer of the ballet *Giselle*, after seeing him in his dual role of dancer and violinist in *Le Violon du Diable*: "I will not say that M. Saint-Léon plays the violin like Paganini, but what I can declare is that if Paganini had danced like M. Saint-Léon, he would certainly not have played the violin as he did. He who was partial to so many pieces on a single string would have found it superflous to add one more to his bow. As a violinist Saint-Léon belongs to the Paganini school. He seeks his principal effects in the eccentricities and the difficulties of harmonics and the succession of *pizzicato* and *col arco*, which does not prevent him from playing with infinite style and elegance the *air varié* and the various *andante* passages of which his musical role is composed. Account must also be taken of the extreme difficulty of taking up the violin in the middle of a scene and playing it at a given moment, without time to make all the preparations that a musician never neglects before starting his solo."[5]

Saint-Léon's musical accomplishments, as violinist

4 *The Times*, 12th May 1843
5 *Le Constitutionnel*, 22nd January 1849

and composer, were to play a prominent part in his achievements as a choreographer. Not only did he sometimes compose passages of music for his own ballets, but he always maintained a very close association with his composer. Also, he was held in considerable esteem as a musician, as the honours he received bear witness: honorary membership of the Accademia Filarmonica Romana and the Società Apollinea of Venice, his appointment in 1844 as Violinist to Marie-Louise, Duchess of Parma, who thirty years before had been Napoleon's second Empress, and the Order of Merit bestowed on him in 1857 by the Duke of Coburg-Gotha.

We must now retrace our steps, for we have digressed from our account of the early appearances of this dual prodigy. A few months after his first concert, on 31st July 1835, Arthur Saint-Léon made his début as a dancer at the Königliches Hof- und National Theater in Munich. Billed as a pupil of his father, he danced in a pas de deux with a Fraulein Scherzer, inserted in Joseph Schneider's ballet *Die reisende Ballet-Gesellschaft* (music by Pentenrieder). Early in 1836 he was dancing in Stuttgart, where his prowess inspired the correspondent of a Viennese paper to write of "the natural grace of all his movements and poses, a proficiency and precision rarely seen at his age, truly astonishing balance, and the most artistic ports de bras."[6]

Léon Michel's appointment at the Court of Württemburg terminated in 1836, and the family returned to Paris. During the next two years Arthur's public appearances were limited to concerts as a violinist in the salons of the French capital, but his main activity was in the studio of Albert, one of the most distinguished teachers of ballet of the time, under whose guidance he industriously strove to perfect his technique as a dancer.

François Decombe, professionally known as Albert,

---

[6] *Bäuerles Theater-Zeitung*, 5th April 1836

was one of the last protagonists of the genre noble or sérieux. He had himself studied under Jean-François Coulon and during the years he had danced at the Opéra, from 1808 to 1832, had been acclaimed for the dignity and majesty of his style. But if his style of dancing was becoming an anachronism in the bourgeois climate of Louis Philippe's reign, he was recognised as one of the most progressive of teachers. Adice credited him and Filippo Taglioni with introducing "a new gymnastic, more scientific, better applied, a well-directed method that discarded none of the principles that were recognised as being excellent, but that added to it new combinations, long, hard and progressive enchaînements, whose results were to form the chest, give control to the legs, and harden the whole body for difficulties, for the most difficult and complicated movements."[7]

Through Albert Saint-Léon obtained his first important engagement in Brussels in 1838-39. This was followed by engagements in Vienna and Milan. His reputation grew steadily, and in 1843 he signed a contract as a principal male dancer at Her Majesty's Theatre, London. There he made an immediate impression. *The Times* acclaimed him as "a wonder in his way. The vigour which he exhibits, the immensity of his pirouettes, and other feats, seem to mark him as the founder of an entirely new school of dancing." "His dancing is the sport of a young Hercules . . . He flings himself about with the most astounding force: we cannot surmise how many times he goes round in a single spin, it seems as though he had given himself an impetus he could not check. Whirled about as a hurricane, he stops as firm as a rock . . . Saint-Léon is a phenomenon."[8]

This first London season was a turning point in his

[7] G. Léopold Adice, *Théorie de la gymnastique de la danse théâtrale* (Paris, 1859), p.83.
[8] *The Times*, 21st and 28th April 1843

career, for it marked the beginning of his partnership with the Neapolitan ballerina, Fanny Cerrito, one of the most fascinating ballet stars of the time, with whom he was to be most closely associated for the next eight years. Their paths had crossed before, in Vienna in 1841, but they had then danced together only once. Now he was to become her regular partner; he joined her in the famous pas de quatre from *Le Lac des fées*, and together they also danced an animated character dance, the Pas Styrien.

They were, of course, most useful to each other, but at the outset it was he who stood to benefit most, for to be attached to a ballerina of Cerrito's standing was a rare opportunity, which he seized with eagerness and devotion. She was four years his elder, and was one of the greatest names in the world of ballet. She was also a beautiful woman, and the impressionable Saint-Léon quickly fell in love with her. For more than a year Cerrito wavered, but on 17th April 1845 they were married at Les Batignolles.

Their partnership falls into two distinct phases: from 1843 to 1847, the year they were engaged at the Paris Opéra; and from 1847 until the year of their separation, 1851. During the first four years their activities centred on London, where they were engaged for the opera season each summer, and Saint-Léon played a secondary role as Cerrito's partner. From their engagement in Paris, however, it became at least an equal partnership, with Saint-Léon assuming also the status of choreographer.

In surveying the years from 1843 to 1847 one is struck by the character dances which appear frequently in their repertory. Cerrito, of course, was not the only ballerina of her period to make use of national and folk dance. Fanny Elssler had already led the way with her Cachucha, and dances of that kind, in varying degrees based on authentic folk originals and stylised for the stage, had become a feature of Romantic ballet. In 1844

14

Cerrito and Saint-Léon brought out the Manola, and this was followed by what was perhaps their most famous character dance, the Redowa Polka. The polka was then the latest craze in the ballroom, and Carlotta Grisi and Jules Perrot had already produced a stage version. The Redowa – puffed as "the original polka of Bohemia" – was a brilliant little sketch of rustic coquetry and gallantry. There is a charming lithograph of Cerrito and Saint-Léon, back to back, in a moment from this dance, but it gives no idea of its infectious humour – the girl's teasing, her "peeping over shoulders, slant looks, mock repulses, nods, winks, and arch recognitions." Other dances of this sort were the Sicilienne in Cerrito's ballet *Rosida*, and, in a more modern vein, the Polka da Sala which they danced in Rome in 1844. Saint-Léon was not credited with the choreography of these dances, but in such a close partnership as theirs it would have been difficult to define where the work of one ended and that of the other began. It is more than likely that he had a hand in creating some of them.

By 1847 the twenty-six-year-old Saint-Léon had become the dominant figure in the partnership. This is evident from his correspondence with the Paris Opéra prior to the couple's engagement in 1847 (Letters 4 to 7). Clearly the Opéra was interested not only in the ballerina, but also in Saint-Léon himself as choreographer. One may surmise that in early exchanges – in letters which preceded those published here – he had persuasively made it a condition of their engagement that he should produce the ballet for their début. He proposed *Alma*, a vehicle specially produced for Cerrito five years before, and came to an arrangement with the ballet composer, Cesare Pugni, to adapt the original score by Michael Costa. It was a typical ploy of Saint-Léon's to offer a "package deal", and the Opéra was clearly grateful to be given a ballet which entailed no great expenditure and could be speedily staged.

In his early choreographic essays Saint-Léon proved his usefulness to Cerrito and to the Opéra. Generally speaking they were ballets made to measure, vehicles for the ballerina, containing tried passages from earlier works to set off Cerrito's particular qualities. *La Fille de marbre* was a revision of *Alma*, including the famous pas de fascination which Perrot had arranged for Cerrito. In *La Vivandière*, a new version of a ballet which had been in their repertory for some years, Saint-Léon inserted the Redowa Polka and the pas de quatre from Guerra's *Le Lac des fées*, transposed into a pas de six. *Le Violon du Diable* was again a revival, having been created earlier in Venice. The highlight of *Stella* was the Sicilienne, another of their successful character dances. *Pâquerette*, Saint-Léon's last ballet for his wife, differed from those which had gone before in that it had a scenario, albeit rather a banal one, by Gautier. It is also noteworthy for containing a Hungarian dance for Cerrito. The couple had visited Pest in 1846, and the riches of Hungarian folklore had obviously made a deep impression on Saint-Léon, for he was to draw on this source several times in his career.

It was with these ballets that Saint-Léon began to acquire his reputation as a choreographer. That he had a facility for arranging dances was not in doubt, but fertile though his imagination was, the process of creation came perhaps a little too easily to him. He was inclined to work hurriedly, and to neglect the dramatic structure of the work. He was also over-concerned with producing the kind of ballet that was expected of him at the expense of giving his imagination full rein. This compliance to the demands of opera directors was to be very helpful to him in his career, but it placed him, as a creative artist, on a lower level than his contemporaries Perrot and Bournonville.

While arranging a brilliant setting for Cerrito's gifts, he did not neglect to provide himself with opportunities. He was still a phenomenal dancer, even if certain physical defects were now becoming more marked, in particular what Charles Maurice called "a prominent shoulder."[9] The Parisians were impressed by the height of his jumps, the power and control of his turns, and his masculine manner. Maurice, however, recognised a certain vulgarity in his technical displays and spoke of his "jumping about after the manner of the Groteschi"[10] – a memory of the acrobatic feats of the Kobblers which had astonished Paris thirty-six years before. But his most spectacular achievement during this period was his appearance as both violinist and dancer in *Le Violon du Diable*.

Saint-Léon and Cerrito separated in 1851, after an engagement in Madrid, and in December of the following year Saint-Léon's contract with the Opéra was terminated at the instance of the Direction on payment of agreed compensation. In his latter time at the Opéra he had been performing the duties of premier maître de ballet, premier danseur and professeur de la classe de perfectionnement, and yet he had found time to perfect a system of dance notation and to write a manual of it which he published privately in 1852 under the title of *La Sténochorégraphie*.

It is of particular importance because it is the first system of dance notation to be based on a visual representation of the human figure. One needs only a glance to get an idea of the movement from the little figures on the paper. Earlier systems, like those of Feuillet, had concentrated on recording the track taken by the dancer and neglected movements of the head, arms and torso. Saint-Leon's choreographic notation is written on six-line staves above the music. The top line, called the shoulder line, is reserved for signs indicating movements of the body and the arms, the five lower lines being for the movements of the feet and legs. This is not the place to analyse the system, but

[9] *Coureur des Spectacles*, 21st October 1847
[10] *Coureur des Spectacles*, 22nd October 1848

credit should be given to this busy man, not only for devising the system, but for his perspicacity in seeing the need for the dance to find a language. In this he was a man well in advance of his time, and his remarks are as apt today as when he wrote them.

"Music, painting, architecture, horsemanship, all the arts in fact," he wrote, "have a language by the aid of which its principles and rules can be reproduced. The DANCE, being based on design and anatomy, also has its principles and rules, but they are only *demonstrable*, for CHOREOGRAPHY properly so-called exists only in name. The cradle of the dance, the Théâtre de l'Opéra, has possessed great artists, ballet-masters of the first order, but what remains of their labours, their works? Nothing apart from the titles of those works and a few *traditions*, more or less exact, handed down by their contemporaries or their pupils, dependent on the intelligence, capability and memory of each of them, and consequently corrupted, incomplete and today almost forgotten . . . In my opinion the art of the *dance* is in its infancy. What in our day it is customary to call, wrongly, CHOREOGRAPHY does not really exist. Indeed what does the word CHOREOGRAPHY really mean? To *write down the dance*, not to *compose it*. But in order to write there must be a method as there is for musical composition, instrumental playing and singing, and to construct this method it is absolutely essential to have a single language, understood by all those who wish to teach or to create usefully and seriously."[11]

To what extent was Saint-Léon's system of notation, which certainly marked a radical departure from earlier systems, original? According to Adice,[12] an Italian who danced for some years at the Paris Opéra and later became a teacher there, Saint-Léon's teacher Albert had

[11] Arthur Saint-Léon, *La Sténochorégraphie* (Paris, 1852), pp. 7 – 9.
[12] G. Léopold Adice, *Notes sur la direction E. Perrin* (MS, Bibliothèque de l'Opéra).

18

had "some idea of telegraphy. Based on that he conceived the idea of applying the plastic movements of the telegraph to the person dancing on the stage by means of the five-line music staff, thinking he had thereby discovered the way to notate the movements of theatrical dancing on paper in the same way as writing modern music. He often spoke of it to his pupils, among whom was Saint-Léon. But when he began to think how to work out the method on which to base his system, he quickly saw that his idea was inadequate in practice, called it nonsense, and soon spoke no more about it." Adice, who harboured a grudge against Saint-Léon, alleged that the latter, out of an ambition to be considered erudite and "remembering all he had heard his teacher say (his retentive memory was his greatest quality . . .) gathered it all for good or ill in a few parts published in instalments, and followed them, quite unnecessarily, by some very imperfect and partial biographies of old ballet-masters."[13]

From this one may conclude that the germ of Saint-Léon's system came from Albert's half-hearted attempts to commit movement to paper by the use of stick figures, but had Albert developed it to anything like the degree which Saint-Léon achieved he would surely not have discarded it as "nonsense." Saint-Léon's system was carefully worked out by a man with a sound musical knowledge and was a significant development in the history of dance notation. Unfortunately, however, he seems to have made only spasmodic use of it. The Paris Opéra Library possesses a répétiteur, ironically of a minor work, *Il Basilico*, which includes, here and there, choreographic notations in his own hand, and

[13] In justice to Saint-Léon the biographies of ballet-masters contain much information that is not to be found elsewhere, but it is true that they contain a number of errors, some of which have been perpetuated by later writers – e.g. the forenames of Beauchamps (Charles Louis instead of Pierre) and the date of the creation of *La Fille mal gardée* (1786 instead of 1789).

also a fair copy of part of the peasant pas de deux from *Giselle*. His surviving letters contain no mention of notation, and one is led to the conclusion that he had no time, or in his later years no energy, for the daunting task of committing his ballets to paper. As recompense, however, he recorded one substantial piece of choreography in full detail, as an illustration of his system for his book – the pas de six from *La Vivandière*, as danced by Cerrito and himself with four supporting danseuses – and it is worthy of note that he honestly gave credit to the fact that it was based on Guerra's choreography for *Le Lac des fées*.

Saint-Léon dedicated his book to the Tsar of Russia, Nicolas I. His motive is not hard to discern. Having broken with Fanny Cerrito, who was ballerina en titre at the Opéra, he was seeking fresh fields to conquer and in this way was staking his claim for the post of ballet-master in Russia, should it become vacant. He was to wait seven years before this opportunity arose.

These seven years were years of bustling activity. In 1853 he arranged the choreography for two opera-ballets at the Théâtre Lyrique in Paris, *Le Lutin de la vallée* and *Le Danseur du roi*, and the following year he was engaged as choreographer and dancer at the São Carlos theatre in Lisbon. Lisbon was very much a minor centre of the dance, but during his two seasons there he wielded exceptional authority and the ballet enjoyed a spell of unusual prosperity. Saint-Léon was accompanied by several dancers who had been with him at the Théâtre Lyrique, including a ballerina who was to be closely associated with him, both professionally and in private life, for the rest of his days. This was Louise Fleury, or Laurent, to give her real name. Some five years younger than he, she too was pupil of Albert, who had developed her strong technique but had not succeeded in overcoming her lack of interpretation. With her tall, slender figure, she had been a regal and somewhat remote Queen of the Wilis in the first

20

London production of *Giselle* in 1842, and had danced at the Paris Opéra from 1843 to 1848.

Saint-Léon's two years in Portugal were very prolific, among the new ballets he produced there being *Saltarello*, *Os Saltimbancos* (which he was to stage elsewhere as *Le Procès du Fandango*) and *Meteora*. He became a Professor of the Lisbon Conservatoire, and in April 1855 he was awarded the Cross of the Order of Christ by the King-Regent, Ferdinand.

However, the affairs of the São Carlos theatre did not prosper, and in February 1856, when the salaries due to him and the dancers fell into arrear, he had to threaten to withhold their services if they were not paid within three days. The management mistakenly assumed he was bluffing, and uproar broke out in the theatre when the dancers failed to appear. For this he spent a short time in the Carmo prison, from which he was released only on the intervention of the French minister.

In spite of this unfortunate incident Saint-Léon's years in Lisbon apparently provided him with the opportunity of testing some of his ideas, which he expounded in a pamphlet published there in 1856, *De l'Etat actuel de la danse*. This little known work gives an interesting insight into his thoughts. It reveals a man who is aware of the decadent features of mid-nineteenth-century ballet and has definite ideas for raising the status of the dance as an art. He opened his treatise by remarking on the inferior place which ballet occupied in the French theatre, where the emptiness of the choreographic material was all too often concealed by spectacular mise-en-scène. There had been a noticeable decline in the artistic content of the dance since the eighteenth century, when dancing was a normal part of a person's education and the public appreciated its finer points. Now a dancer had to struggle to make an impression, and this had been a cause of the lack of good dancers in the 1850s. In the recent past there had been only four outstanding stars – Taglioni, Elssler, Cerrito and Carlotta Grisi. Taglioni

21

had not danced better than her predecessors, but she had created a new type of dancer through the poetry and simplicity of her style and the flowing grace of her movements. Her success, however, had the unfortunate consequence of concentrating attention on the ballerina. Choreographers no longer troubled about the ensemble. They had abdicated their preeminence not only because of the dominance of the star ballerina, but also because of the appearance of the scenarist as a co-author. There had been a marked decline since the early part of the century when choreographers such as Viganò and Gioja could create a ballet as an entity in itself, not only devising the plot and arranging the action, but also composing or arranging the music so as to achieve the full effect they desired. In the mid-nineteenth century, on the other hand, a choreographer was often a second-rate dancer with no musical knowledge and lacking in ideas or taste. A brilliant executant himself, Saint-Léon also deplored the lack of strong male dancers.

In his view the only way to regenerate the ballet was to establish serious teaching institutions and produce choreographers in the full sense of the term. To rectify the over-emphasis on the ballerina he pressed for a better drilled corps de ballet. He had been very impressed by the children's ballet companies of Horschelt and Frau Weiss, and recommended a special, quasi-military training, in which a corps de ballet dancer would be specially trained to be part of a well drilled ensemble. All corps de ballet dancers would be equal in importance, so that the whole would not be spoilt by individual ambition. He clearly envisaged that, given a greater respect accorded to the corps de ballet, a dancer of the corps would feel pride in being part of a team. In Lisbon he had attempted to put these ideas into practice, and the experiment, he felt, had revealed the advantages and had "almost put an end to the choreographic *cacophony* that had previously existed."[14]

[14] Arthur Saint-Léon, *De l'Etat actuel de la danse* (Lisbon, 1856), p. 13

22

Specialised corps de ballet training would find its place in his ideal Conservatoire de la Danse, in which music would be taught as an integral part of a dancer's training and, most important of all, order would be introduced into the training method. This was where his system of notation came in. "The art of the dance is all the more difficult in that it does not have, as do all the others, a *language* of its own and consequently lacks the means by which a pupil can make regular studies and gather the fruit of the great masters who bequeath only memories or traditions that are of doubtful authenticity. The dance is therefore taught, so to speak, by heart and the pupil is at the mercy of the often dubious ability of the teacher who demonstrates what he believes to be good, who has his own principles that are always different from those of his colleagues, and who has no method before his eyes to guide him, with the result that far from setting the pupil on the right road, he leads him astray by work that is damaging to his talent."[15]

These ideas had to be put aside after his departure from Lisbon, for Saint-Léon embarked on an arduous tour lasting nearly eighteen months: Vienna, Turin, Königsberg, Tilsit, Pest, Temesvar, Dresden, Stuttgart, Munich, Augsberg, Magdeburg, Brunswick. It was apparently a highly successful venture: he travelled with Louise Fleury as his ballerina and companion, carrying around costumes for a small repertory of ballets which he could quickly stage on arrival at a new town, and was usually able to demand half the gross takings.

While touring the cities of Germany Saint-Léon conceived the ambition of moving eastward into Poland and Russia, and he wrote to his agent setting out his proposals (Letter 19). He realised that there could be no thought of St. Petersburg, for Perrot was firmly established there; but Moscow, Warsaw, Odessa and Bucarest seemed to be possibilities. There was no immediate result of this approach, but in less than a year Saint-Léon

[15] Arthur Saint-Léon, *De l'Etat actuel de la danse*, p. 8

was appointed to the post of ballet-master of the Imperial Theatres, which he was to hold from 1859 until his death.

Saint-Léon arrived in St. Petersburg just a year after the visit which Théophile Gautier described in such vivid detail in his *Voyage en Russie*. Through Gautier's words we can visualise the city Saint-Léon would have known. In those early years under Alexander II Russia was enjoying a brief relaxation of the repression which the previous Tsar, Nicolas I, had imposed; contacts with the outside world multiplied, and many visitors from Western Europe were surprised to find in St. Petersburg a society in which, in its upper strata, they could feel so much at home, not least because French was spoken "by every Russian of any distinction." Gautier described his experiences with the superficial eye of a tourist, and made no comment on the appalling social problems that Russia was then facing. In 1861 the serfs were emancipated, but this epoch-making measure did not cure the malaise that was slowly but inexorably destroying the structure of Russian society: the grip of the bureaucracy had lost little of its debilitating force, and a spreading discontent, stimulated by new contacts with the West and directed not so much against the Tsar as against the system, was crystallising in underground societies dedicated to overthrowing the regime. Saint-Léon, whose post was virtually a Court appointment, could not ignore these sinister undercurrents, and in one of his letters (Letter 42) he gave a penetrating glimpse of the Tsar wrestling with the problem of whether to pardon a young rebel.

To Saint-Léon such matters were incidental, for he was clearly little interested in politics. His world was the dance, and at this moment of his career the ballet company of the Bolshoi Theatre in St. Petersburg absorbed his full attention, much as it had fascinated Gautier. The latter, with his critic's judgment and his wide knowledge of the theatre and the ballet, had noted

24

several features. "Opera and ballet are not given at the Italian Opera in St. Petersburg in the same performance," he explained. "They are two entirely separate presentations, each having its exclusive days . . . Since the dance has to make up an entire programme, ballets are much more developed than they are with us; they have anything up to four or five acts, with many scenes and scene changes, or else two are given in the same performance . . . The Russians are great connoisseurs of ballets, and the volleys of their opera-glasses are formidable. Whoever has survived them has confidently arrived. Their Ballet School turns out remarkable soloists and a corps de ballet that is unequalled for its ensemble and precision, and the rapidity of its evolutions . . . This corps de ballet is carefully chosen from among the pupils of the School. Many of them are pretty, all are young and well formed, and all have studied their craft – or their art, if you prefer – seriously."[16]

This was the milieu in which Saint-Léon found himself assuming the mantle of Jules Perrot. Perrot, who had been ballet-master in Russia, with one short interval, since 1848, had earned the reputation of being, in Gautier's phrase, "a choreographer without a rival." His ballets were an impressive combination of dance and drama, and in the company of Russian dancers in St. Petersburg he had discovered ideal material to translate his imaginative ideas into action on the stage. As the years passed, however, he had become increasingly unhappy, conceivably because of the restrictive supervision exercised by the Direction of the Imperial Theatres, which in a land where tight censorship had for so long been the rule was prone to see subversive tendencies in the most innocent places. His "persistent illness", whether it was diplomatic or psychosomatic, led the Direction to take the view that he was unreliable

[16] Théophile Gautier, *Voyage en Russie* (Paris, 1867), pp. 249-251

25

and to look for a successor. Thus Saint-Léon had his opportunity, being engaged originally as ballet-master in Moscow but with a stipulation that he could be called upon to take on similar duties in St. Petersburg if the need arose, as indeed it did when Perrot withdrew.

Saint-Léon was to hold the post of ballet-master of the Imperial Theatres for eleven successive seasons – from 1859-60 to 1869-70 – and since his duties in Russia occupied only about half the year, he was at liberty to spend many of the intervening summers working as guest choreographer at the Paris Opéra. In this way he became the dominant figure of both Russian and French ballet during the greater part of the 1860s.

At that time it was the custom in St. Petersburg to feature a foreign celebrity in the ballet, and Saint-Léon's first assignment was to produce *Jovita* for the Italian ballerina Carolina Rosati. This could hardly count as an original work, for there was probably no question of changing the choreography of the title-role, which Rosati had created in Paris six years before, and Saint-Léon's task must have been limited to arranging the action and a certain amount of new ensemble work. From then on, however, his work in Russia was his own, some ballets being entirely new, and others being reworkings of ballets he had produced elsewhere. He has been criticised for producing old ballets under new titles, but it hardly seems fair to damn him for renaming a work when it was adapted for a different stage and a company of different temperament and quality, making no secret of its origin.

Being both willing and reliable, Saint-Léon knew how to satisfy the Direction of the Imperial Theatres and the balletomanes who wielded much power in matters of taste. This question of taste is central to judging his calibre as a choreographer, for his tendency to adapt his creative gifts to the taste of his employers instead of following the dictates of his imagination was undeniably a weakness. Nevertheless he was very much

26

a man of his time, and if his ballets lacked the strong dramatic thread that had distinguished the works of Perrot, the majority of the ballet-going public asked for little more than what he provided – brilliant dance numbers, colourful settings, and ingenious and fantastic stage effects, in short visual delights which made no great demands either on the emotions or on the intellect of the spectator.

Saint-Léon's ballets were rich in dancing, being packed with classical variations, often of great technical difficulty, ingenious ensembles, and an astonishing variety of character dances. His interest in national dances had served him well and often in his partnership with Cerrito, and was to supply him with a flood of material when he was ballet-master in Russia. He was by no means the first choreographer to seek inspiration from folk sources, but none had made such lavish and extensive use of this material before. He had travelled widely, and the basic content of many of his character dances must have been genuine enough, even if at times his understanding of the originals may have been somewhat superficial. Italian, Spanish, Flemish, Scottish dances all found their way into his ballets, and in *Koniok Gorbunok* (*Le Petit Cheval bossu*) he boldly attempted a ballet on a Russian theme with a divertissement of dances of Russian character.

In the process of creation Saint-Léon was exceptionally sensitive to the personality and the qualities of the ballerina. He needed an interpreter who was sympathetic to his ideas, and he must have soon been led to consider the respective merits of two brilliant young ballerinas who were on the threshold of greatness, Marfa Muravieva and Praskovia Lebedeva. They were almost exact contemporaries – Muravieva was twenty-one when Saint-Léon arrived in Russia, Lebedeva about a year younger – and they were both Moscow-born. Muravieva, however, had been trained in the Theatre School of St. Petersburg, while Lebedeva had remained

27

in Moscow, and this circumstance had served to heighten the contrast between their styles: Muravieva's outstanding qualities were her musicality and technical virtuosity, while Lebedeva was above all a dramatic ballerina. Both dancers had risen quickly to the front rank: Muravieva was appointed to soloist rank immediately after graduating from the Theatre School, while Lebedeva was dancing the roles of Giselle, Catarina and Esmeralda in Moscow at the age of sixteen.

Saint-Léon's preference was for Muravieva, whom he chose to create the title-role in *Théolinde* in 1862. He accompanied her on her two visits to Paris, in 1863 and 1864, and produced *Diavolina* and *Néméa* for her at the Opéra. Her last creation was the part of the Tsar-Maiden in his *Koniok Gorbunok* in 1864. Shortly after this she abandoned the stage to marry.

Saint-Léon's relationship with Lebedeva was not so happy. Their basic concepts were too much at variance. She was transferred to St. Petersburg in 1865, and it was for her that he began work on *Le Poisson doré*. The personal differences that arose during the production can be sensed from Saint-Léon's letters. Lebedeva's unhappiness about the form of the ballet was matched by the disheartening effect which her attitude had on the choreographer during its long gestation period. Even before the first part of the ballet was presented at a gala Saint-Léon told Nuitter that Lebedeva "is going to kill my new ballet which I am beginning without any enthusiasm" (Letter 38), and later, when she suffered an eye injury and rehearsals had to be suspended, he despairingly referred to it as "my unbearable ballet" (Letter 51). Shortly afterwards Lebedeva asked to be released from her contract, and although ill health was the reason she gave, a contemporary report revealed that "a lack of good will on the part of the Direction in the case of the production of *Le Poisson doré*" was the "sad fact" that had prompted her retirement.[17]

[17] *Peterburgsky Listok*, 1st March 1867 (old style)

28

Lebedeva, who perhaps felt out of her element in St. Petersburg, might very understandably have been distressed by Saint-Léon's enthusiastic support of Adèle Grantzow, who had been engaged on his recommendation to take her place in Moscow. The twenty-year-old Grantzow was then almost completely unknown. The daughter of a minor German ballet-master, Gustav Grantzow, she had attracted Saint-Léon's notice in Hanover and shortly afterwards had gone to Paris to complete her training under Mme. Dominique, the teacher of Emma Livry and many other French dancers of the time. Although her biographer said that she went to Paris at her own expense, it is possible that Saint-Léon himself provided the required financial assistance.[18] He must have followed her progress under Mme. Dominique very closely to have recommended her for the important post of principal ballerina in Moscow when her stage experience was limited to a few appearances in Brunswick and Hanover. His instinct did not let him down, for she exceeded all his expectations of her. The letter he wrote to Mme. Dominique describing her début (Letter 30) shows him in a mood of exaltation. "I am mad about her," he exclaimed. "Always having to deal with dancers whose mechanism has to be concealed, it is good to have a merry little girl who possesses everything."

In Adèle Grantzow he seemed to have found an ideal interpreter, richly endowed with beauty, intelligence and a technique of staggering power. Her triumphs in Moscow and St. Petersburg in the winter of 1865-66

[18] *Le Gaulois* (15th June 1877), in reporting her death, wrote: "The theatre director from Moscow, who had the opportunity of seeing her in *Robert le Diable* in Hanover, paid for the completion of her dance training and sent her to Paris, where she was taught by Mme. Dominique." It is hardly likely that a Russian theatre director would have sent her to Paris, but quite understandable that Saint-Léon would have subsidised her journey to study under his old friend, Mme. Dominique. At that time, of course, there was no question of any vacancy in Russia.

were followed, in the summer of 1866, by a no less successful début at the Paris Opéra. Not only could Saint-Léon feel satisfaction at seeing his faith in his protégée so fully justified, but as a choreographer he found a new source of inspiration. But alas, the splendour of Grantzow's early promise was soon to be dimmed by injury and illness. Although it was for her that Saint-Léon was to conceive *La Source* and *Coppélia*, she was not to create either of them. Bad luck dogged her to the end of her days, for her premature death, at the age of thirty-two, was to be the result of gross medical negligence.

Most of Saint-Léon's letters collected here date from the last five years of his life. Because they were written to his Parisian scenarist, Charles Nuitter, they deal most fully with the two works he produced at the Opéra, *La Source* (1866) and *Coppélia* (1870), and refer only briefly to the ballets he was producing in St. Petersburg, *Le Poisson doré* (1866-67) and *Le Lys* (1869). Nuitter was Saint-Léon's lifeline to Paris, and their correspondence played an important part in the production of *La Source* and *Coppélia*. To have such a faithful and devoted correspondent – "you who are so prompt and keep your word to the end" was Saint-Léon's own tribute (Letter 50) – was compensation for all the frustrations which he had to endure in their preparation.

La Source was originally planned to crown Grantzow's first Paris season, in 1866, but owing first to a foot injury, and then to the decision to expand the ballet, it was not ready by the time she had to return to Russia. Great efforts were made to obtain an extension of leave for both herself and Saint-Léon, but the Russian authorities would not release them because of the festivities for the Tsarevitch's wedding. So Saint-Léon had the doubly galling experience of being unable to supervise the final rehearsals of his ballet and having to accept a last-minute replacement for the ballerina for whom he had conceived the main role. This was Guglielmina

Saint-Léon, the dancer-violinist, in *Le Violon du Diable* (1849), with
his wife Fanny Cerrito. (Bibl. de l'Opéra)

Saint-Léon, the virtuoso dancer, in *Pâquerette* (1851).
Caricature by Marcelin, from the *Journal pour rire*
of 14th February 1851.

A page from Saint-Léon's *La Sténochorégraphie*, showing part of the
coda of the *pas de six* from *La Vivandière* (1848) recorded in his
system of dance notation.

Saint-Léon in 1863. Photograph by Bergamasco of St. Petersburg.
(Collection of Ivor Guest)

Salvioni, who danced and mimed in a forceful Italian style and lacked Grantzow's fluidity and charm. At a distance of more than a thousand miles Saint-Léon could only hope that all would go well. His anxiety was increased by his lack of confidence in Salvioni, and he would have been happier if the ballet had been postponed to the following summer. "Until the ballet is given, keep me in touch with everything, make this sacrifice for me," he begged (Letter 38), and Nuitter seems to have done just that. Saint-Léon knew that the ballet could only be properly judged when Grantzow appeared as Naila, and his consolation came when she triumphantly took over the role in the summer of 1867 and virtually created it anew.

Similar ill fortune attended *Le Poisson doré* which he was preparing at the same time in St. Petersburg. It was created in patches, and plagued by the unconcealed dissatisfaction of Lebedeva, for whom it was originally intended. Her retirement caused nearly a year's delay before the complete work was presented, and once again the replacement was Salvioni, who predictably made little impression.

Saint-Léon's last production in Russia, *Le Lys*, based on a Chinese theme, was also a failure. According to his own account (Letters 59 and 60) Grantzow enjoyed a personal success in it and the Tsar expressed his pleasure, but the work had given Saint-Léon more trouble than any other ballet he had produced and, like its predecessor, it disappeared quickly and unregretted from the repertory. Almost its only point of interest to us today was a character dance called "La Bamboula", which may have been inspired by Louis Moreau Gottschalk's piano piece, famous for its cakewalk rhythm. Gottschalk and Saint-Léon were both virtuosi, and it is conceivable that the two met, and found much in common, when the American composer had visited France some twenty years earlier.

That Saint-Léon no longer had his heart in his tasks in

Russia is clear from his letters and also perhaps from the quality of his choreography for *Le Lys*. But despite his deteriorating health, he had not lost his sense of dedication nor his master's touch. He may have been disillusioned with Russia, but the dance was still the mainspring of his existence, and all his thoughts and energy were being directed to the new ballet he was preparing for the Opéra. For this he could not have had more congenial collaborators than Nuitter and Léo Delibes. Between the three of them there arose a close understanding, and Saint-Léon's authority was willingly accepted by the other two. In this ballet, *Coppélia*, Saint-Léon was to produce, for the first time in his career, a ballet that was a balanced piece of theatre, in which scenario, choreography and music were all welded together to produce a homogeneous whole. Its first two scenes, in which virtually the whole of the action takes place, constituted a light comedy ballet of near-perfect construction, with a soubrette role for the ballerina that not even the greatest dancers have scorned ever since. Its one shortcoming was that the final divertissement had little bearing on the plot, but being placed at the end it could be omitted simply and without any rearrangement of the rest of the work. In Nuitter and Delibes, Saint-Léon appeared to have found ideal partners, and it is one of those cruel ironies of Fate that this was to be his last ballet.

The active preparations for *Coppélia* were spread over three summers. Delibes took time and care in writing the score, and if Saint-Léon now and then expressed impatience in his letters to Nuitter, he was certainly very happy with the result. Being a musician himself, he must have been well aware of Delibes' superiority over such composers as Pinto, Pugni and Minkus, with whom he had worked for most of his choreographic career. Delibes' score for *Coppélia* set new standards in ballet composition; it commanded respect on its own merits, and far from being a mere accompaniment to the

32

action, it illustrated it, added tone and colour, and emphasised its meaning and effect. All this Saint-Léon must have sensed and appreciated, although his old habits probably died hard. He was accustomed to dictating his requirements to Minkus, with whom he used to stay when visiting Moscow, and he was frequently, it seems, making suggestions to Delibes: he proposed the form of a variation for Salvioni in *La Source* and even offered to send a "sketch" (Letter 37), and it was he who suggested the thème slave in Act I of *Coppélia* – to Delibes' later discomfiture, it must be added, for the theme turned out to be not of folk origin, as Saint-Léon had imagined, but by the Polish composer Moniuszko!

Another cause of delay in the production of *Coppélia* was the illness of Grantzow, for whom the ballet was originally planned. Fortunately the work was then still in a formative stage, and Saint-Léon was able to reshape it for Giuseppina Bozzacchi, an enchanting young pupil of Mme. Dominique, who was to make her professional début by creating the role of Swanilda. It is a pity that Saint-Léon made no reference in his letters to this young ballerina – who was to die so soon after her triumph, during the Siege of Paris – for we know that he watched over her with paternal solicitude and, some weeks after her début, placed his summer house at Enghien at her disposal so that she could rest in the country air. It was for her that he had given the role of Swanilda its final form, in which it has been faithfully handed down at the Paris Opéra. The additional delay had also enabled him to reflect on the production and tighten up the action so effectively that it has proved virtually impossible to cut or rearrange.

So Saint-Léon came back to Paris in 1870 to savour his last and greatest triumph, *Coppélia*, which was created at the Opéra at the end of May. No doubt he, and others too, looked forward to a long and fruitful association with the Opéra, but that was not to be. For

33

some years his health had been disintegrating, and it was a miracle that in his physical condition he could still produce a masterpiece so light-hearted and charming. In his younger days he had enjoyed good health, suffering only from minor ailments such as rheumatism, for which he took the waters at Bath in 1847 (Letter 7), and this had given him more than a fair share of energy. As well as dancing and devising ballets, he concerned himself with all details of the production as well as musical matters, he coached his ballerinas, and he was capable of managing his own company. If he grumbled about his "position of a galley slave" (Letter 18), it was his life and he would surely have had it no other way. But in 1866, exhausted by the demands made on him in Russia and frustrated at being unable to supervise the final rehearsals of *La Source* in Paris, his health began to fail. It was a moral as well as a physical crisis. "How I loathe my profession," he confessed to Nuitter (Letter 44). Assailed by rheumatism, headaches and stomach trouble, he began to find his duties a burden. By the winter of 1868-69 he was enduring "unbelievable pain" from "a complicated disease of the kidneys and the intestines," and for two and a half months he was able to sleep only for short periods crouched up in an armchair (Letter 57). Depression and fatigue took a heavy toll, and in the last summer of his life, 1870, he was a man grown old before his time.

Two weeks after the first night of *Coppélia* he went, on doctor's advice, to Wiesbaden to take the waters. The Franco–Prussian War broke out shortly after his return to Paris, and as the time for his return to St. Petersburg approached, news of heavy defeats and withdrawals was reaching Paris. The end came with merciful suddenness. He collapsed with a heart attack in the Café du Divan, in the Passage de l'Opéra, on the evening of 2nd September 1870, and was dead before his friends could bring him back to his home in the rue de Laval, where he lived with Louise Fleury.

34

It was the end of an era in more senses than one. The Opéra had just closed for the duration of the war, and would not reopen until the following year, after France's defeat, the fall of the Second Empire, and the holocaust of the Commune. The great flowering of ballet, which had reached its peak under the influence of Romanticism in the 1830s and 1840s but had continued, with diminishing strength, until 1870, had passed. The repertory of those years was to disappear as its ballets, with only one exception, were forgotten. The exception was *Coppélia*, which has survived to enchant us still, one of the last brilliant flames of the Second Empire, reflecting all the confident gaiety of that vanished age, and a lively and fitting memorial to its creator, Arthur Saint-Léon.

THE LETTERS

1

To an Unidentified Correspondent

Dear Sir,

I do not know how to reply to your two letters, and if I heeded only my modesty, you would receive no reply at all. However, I am allowing myself to be led by that little devil pride, to whom our human weakness can refuse hardly anything, and sending you, as a very feeble tribute, an extract from the sixth *Caprice Romantique,* which I have composed.

Please be assured of my high regard for you.

Arthur Saint-Léon

London, 20/6/43

2

To Benjamin Lumley[1]

My dear Sir,

You will surely appreciate that I cannot dance the pas de trois with these two ladies, if I do not have another pas in the evening with the première danseuse. If I did so in *Esmeralda,* it was because I afterwards danced with La

37

Grisi. Do not think me ungracious, but tomorrow I would not give the impression of being *premier danseur*, since M. Perrot would be playing the role, M. Montessu would be dancing the *pas* with Mlle. Elssler, and I would only be in third place. Forgive me, dear Sir, if I cannot make this change, but I am sure you will understand.

Ever your devoted

A. Saint-Léon

The 17th.

3

To Benjamin Lumley[1]

My dear Sir,

Yesterday I spoke to my wife about your request, and I think we can be here on 15th April by giving up a tour in Germany which is being prepared, but if you want to enter into a new arrangement, I must tell you that I could no longer accept the same fee in view of the fact I earn less here than anywhere else. The increase I ask for is £32.10.0 a month, and I assure you that I can make no change in this. So far as my wife is concerned, as she promised when you negotiated the last engagement, she asks no alteration in her share, except that she wishes to be entirely exempt from Income Tax[2] starting from the year '46, and also *for the two of us* for the following years, and if you wish us to be here on 15th April, one fifteenth must be paid to us on account of our fee.

Please accept our kindest regards.

Yours ever,

Arthur Saint-Léon

To Henry Duponchel[1]

My dear Sir,

Enclosed you will find the scenario of the ballet *Alma*[2] in English which I have only been able to send you today, as there was no post yesterday, Sunday. I think it will be easy for you to have it translated, although I find it very incomplete. When you send me a note of the changes you want to make, I will give you more precise details. I think it should be divided into not more than four scenes and two acts; in the English scenario there are six[3], but when I have staged this ballet in different towns I have always done so in four scenes, which is enough to link the principal dances. In the first scene we have the pas de l'animation by Alma and the daughters of fire, in the second the pas de fascination, and in the third the pas de trois and a pas de genre for her alone.[4] After the dances of the third act I conclude the action in the ballroom itself, and when Alma declares her love for Emazor, the room collapses and the first set comes into view with Alma turned back into a statue.

In conclusion I beg you to give your attention and good taste to something that has always worked badly, namely the statue in the first act that has to conceal the ballerina. This statue is set on a rock in the middle of the stage, and at a beat of a gong the statue breaks and reveals Alma coming to life; at the end the effect is reversed when she becomes a statue again. When Alma comes to life a light from above must shine on her alone, beginning green, changing imperceptibly to yellow, and ending bright red for the moment when she comes to life. As for the other effects, they pose no difficulty and are very simple, except the collapse at the end. I look forward to receiving a letter from you with the changes needed in the scenario, which is in too good hands for me to worry.

Please accept my kindest regards,

Yours ever,

A. Saint-Léon

A thousand good wishes from my wife and her family, and our kind regards to M. Escudier.[5]

2nd August 1847

5

To Henri Duponchel

My dear Sir,

Following a letter from M. Deligny[1] in which he asks me, on your behalf, for a somewhat detailed description of the sets for *Alma*, I hasten to write to enclose this. Please let me have your comments on anything I have not clearly explained, and also on the dimensions in the scenery plans which I have had to do by guesswork, not knowing the depth of the stage at the Opéra. These can be adjusted proportionately, always bearing in mind the need to leave plenty of stage area for the dances.

Ever your devoted

A. Saint-Léon

A thousand good wishes from my wife

10.8.47 London

To Henri Duponchel

Bath, 1st Sept. 1847[1]

My dear Sir,

I received M. Deligny's letter at Plymouth and found the changes very helpful, just as I expected having entrusted the scenario to yourself and M. Deligny. There is only one thing to add so as not to have to change the whole of the second act – it is absolutely essential that Periphète should have a diabolical or supernatural power to give meaning to the scenes and the pas de fascination. Perhaps it should be arranged that Periphète should sell or give his soul to the God of Fire for Alma to be brought to life. In one way or another it will be very easy for M. Deligny to make this one little change. As for Costa's music, it is very fine and I shall try and keep as much of it as possible. M. Deligny tells me there are some very distinguished and spirited composers in Paris, which I do not doubt for a moment, but I have already come to an arrangement with Pugni[2], who will come to Paris with me. As I shall have to arrange our pas for the Paris orchestra, it will be more convenient to have the maestro with me.

I doubt if a Parisian composer would be agreeable to making the adjustments that will be necessary on this occasion. I shall be leaving for Paris on Monday or Tuesday at the latest, and will set to work immediately. My wife asks me to send a thousand good wishes to you, and begs you to convey kind regards to M. Deligny from both of us.

Ever your devoted
A. Saint-Léon

Bath 1/9/47

To Eugène Deligny

My dear Deligny,

I have received your kind letter in which you propose, on behalf of the Directors, that our engagement should not begin until 15th September for reasons that I find very reasonable.[1] Indeed I find them so reasonable that I think it would be more advantageous not to begin until 1st October. I shall be in Paris at the end of this month unless I spend a week at some spa to wage war on the rheumatism that has visited me, encouraged by the Siberian weather that has dogged us in this charming city. So we shall shortly see each other again, not any longer as royalists but as nationalists,[2] and I hope that our feeble talents combined with our zeal will bring back as much as possible of the good receipts of Autumn '47. My wife is very well in spite of the steeplechases that Lumley is pleased to make the ladies dance in the name of ballet.[3] She asks me to send thousands and thousands of good wishes to you, as well as to MM. Duponchel and Roqueplan,[4] and looking forward to our little chats, with you rolling your cigarettes and me filling my pipe, remember me to those gentlemen and believe me.

Your devoted friend,

A. Saint-Léon

8

To Pierre-Alfred Ravel[1]

My dear Ravel,

I am extremely sorry that I have to decline the request that you made me this morning, because the reason why we have asked for three months leave is my wife's health, and her doctor whom I consulted this evening has expressly forbidden me to allow her to dance no matter where for a month. If your benefit had been taking place in about October we should be at your service. Another time, therefore, I hope to have the pleasure of rendering you this small service.

With our sincere regrets, believe us,

Yours ever,

A. Saint-Léon

9

The Dance does not admit mediocrity. It attains either the ideal or charlatanism.

Arthur Saint-Léon

Fanny Cerrito-St.-Léon

1850, Paris

10

To Nestor Roqueplan

Paris, 17th Dec. 1852

A complication having arisen in M. Saint-Léon's indisposition forces him to request M. Roqueplan to kindly send a doctor from the theatre as soon as possible.

To M. Roqueplan, Director of the Opéra.

11

To Leroy[1]

Paris 17th Dec. 1852

My dear Leroy,

My indisposition is aggravated by a serious injury to my back. I beg you to send immediately a doctor from the theatre to certify that I am not able to dance this evening.

Ever yours,

A. Saint-Léon

12

To Leroy

Académie Nationale de Musique, Paris, 20th December
[1852]

My dear Leroy,

With reference to the proposals you have made me on behalf of M. Roqueplan, I agree to the termination of my contract with effect from today on the following conditions, namely that I shall be paid my salary for December plus 2,000 francs at the end of January and 2,000 francs at the end of February, as compensation.[1] In your reply, please let me have your written agreement to the above conditions.[2]

Ever yours,

A. Saint-Léon

Paris
58 rue des Martyrs

13

To Gabriele Yella[1]

My dear ladies,

We are having a little picnic this evening at Vachette's where we shall all gather to seek for our stomachs the harmony of the dance studio. I expect you, ladies, at 6 o'clock sharp at Aubry's restaurant, Faubourg Montmartre at the corner of the Boulevard - ask for the room reserved by M. Saint-Léon.

If you do not come I shall see that the music is out of tune for the coda of the pas Espagnol in all the coming performances.

Awaiting your reply.

Yours ever,

A. Saint-Léon

14

To G. B. Benelli[1]

My dear Benelli,

I received your last letter yesterday and I reply to it today, particularly because I have news to tell you. Yesterday evening *La Cenerentola* was given with Alboni, its first performance.[2] Many people were there, but in spite of Alboni's undeniable talent, there was some hissing and the public was very displeased with the opera and the performers. The Lisbon public is insupportable. There is a Spanish tenor[3] who had a success in *La Somnambule*[4], but was hissed yesterday. Forti[5] has sung in *Lucia*[6] and in truth, and without being indulgent, he was not bad, but the public would have nothing to do with him, and he was continually hissed. He is leaving shortly for Italy.

On the 29th we made our début in *Saltarello le Dansomane* which I have arranged from *Le Danseur du Roi*[7]. The success was immense, the victory all the greater because the public claimed that I no longer danced. Fleury was charming, Lisereux too, Marmet very agreeable although hissed because she has a lover in the French embassy!! Lequine was successful, Navarre too. In short I was recalled 5 times, and people are talking of nothing else but my ballet in the beautiful but stupid city of Lisbon.[8] You see I have completely changed my tactics after finding the public so capricious. I chose the *Dansomane*, which is a sure success. *Le Violon du Diable* would be a fiasco here, *Ondine* would bring murder on our heads too. One must beware of these gentlemen. We are appearing on Friday and I am preparing a divertissement for Alboni's performances. It will be performed by Lisereux.

Alboni must appear in another opera immediately in which she has more singing. At least there were cries of encore for the Rondo, but she did not want to repeat it, because she was very displeased with the public. Let us hope that all this will work out. Swift[9] has arrived from Oporto for *Puritani*[10], he was tolerated, no more.

I recommend you to speak to York[11] about the difference in my salary, it is enormous for me, and together with your fees it reduces my salary by 16 per cent. It is immense.

I cannot advise York too much about his own business, 1st because he does not ask my advice, and 2ndly because it is something which you cannot do by halves. In ballet my task is to make the thing run well. Fleury was very much liked for her figure, her distinction and her beautiful dancing. Lisereux enchanted everyone by her vivacity. *Le Violon* made an impression although the Adagio is not liked here!!!!!!!!!!!!!!!!

46

Farewell, my dear Benelli. You have not told me if Vandris has been engaged?[12] Awaiting your next,

I am, yours ever,

A. Saint-Léon

Lisbon, 1st November 1854
Largo San Carlos 1

15

To G. B. Benelli

My dear Benelli,

I have been putting off writing to you from day to day just as people put off paying me from day to day, for, to be frank, I do not have a penny and if disaster were to strike the theatre tomorrow, which is still likely at any time, I should hardly have enough to get away. I have incurred great expense setting myself up here, and my rent has to be paid in advance for the whole year, 1,200 francs, which is not dear but it has made things tight for me. Now there is something else. York claims that I have to give him your money, because you have received a sum of 3,000 francs or so which you owe him, and when I was last paid 250 fr. was deducted in your name. Try and sort all this out. People are saying that the theatre is to have a new management. M. Orta has put M. Corsadi Visconti in charge to look after his interests.[1]

Alboni was liked in *La Favorita*[2] and *La Sonnanbula*. The Box Office receipts are good for each new opera, but they do not keep up. Subsequent performances show a steep decline. *Anna Bolena*[3] is being put on for her. On Saturday I give *Les Abeilles* and the 1ère of *Le Lutin* as a ballet. I am to be paid in five days time – we shall see – but I beg you to be patient, first by settling matters between yourself and York, for otherwise I shall be the victim. I continue to lose not 10% but 11!!! It is monstrous. I ought to have done very well. I have handed your letter to York, and am looking for M. Peyremond, but nobody has heard of him. I hope I shall find him.

Saltarello is still the rage. *Lia*, a short ballet, has been *'pateade'* (hissed) at the 4th performance as a result of the stupidity of the management, which always gives the grand ballet with Alboni and me only once or twice a week for the subscribers. They hiss everything except the grand ballet. In *Les Abeilles* I dance only very little (one day *Saltarello* another *Les Abeilles*), and as I have to dance every day as compensation, I always lose the 11%. The new management is talking of dismissing everybody.

Try and arrange something good for me in Rio, Mexico and North America. With 5 or 6 persons and as many works. I would like to go on a tour of those countries, but for a fee for each performance. I would willingly agree to two years for that. I cannot do anything about Paris. I do not know M. Crosnier, and it is not for me to make a proposal.[4] Furthermore, I do not know whether they want anything more than the choreographic works they already possess.

The management of the theatre here has been indirectly offered to me, but the public is too peculiar for me to have any thought of accepting such a task. Others can have this pleasure.[5]

Finally, please sort out the matter with York. I await a decision.

Yours ever,

A. Saint-Léon

13th December 1854

Lisbon
Largo San Carlos, No. 1

48

To G. B. Benelli

My dear Benelli,

I am so busy, tired and harassed that I neglect everything, even my parents and my own interests. I fully understand, however, that you are waiting for me to send you the rest of the "Censeria" but it is also essential that we come to an understanding and that you reach an understanding with M. York. He claims he has an agreement with you under which you owe him half the fare. When I showed him the note of your expenses he showed me another according to which you still owe him 16 fr. because you did not acknowledge having received a sum of 3,000 fr. which he sent you. All this, please note, does not concern me at all, but I am telling you this to show that I have been looking after your interests. As I have a contract with York, I cannot remit any sum unless you give me an authority to pay through M. York. So far he has received or deducted a sum of 250 fr. as a provisional retention until the matter has been settled.

If I had not been on my guard I would have already parted with the whole sum to York. It was in your interests that I refused to do this, and consequently I expect the problem to be resolved. I am between the hammer and the anvil. You ask me for the fare, and York formally objects to it. Eleven per cent is still being withheld and I doubt whether I shall receive a penny of it. We have all been cheated. And if you remember I had said as much in Paris when I was told I would be paid in English money – which was eventually done, but at a rate of 27 fr.25 to the £ sterling – you will see what a joke that was! I repeat, my dear Benelli, come to an arrangement with York, for it does not matter to me whether payment is made from one side or the other. The theatre is now running well, many reforms have been made. My ballets are all the rage. *Le Lutin* and *Les*

Tribulations de Zefferini, the Carnival ballet, are drawing good houses. This makes 6 ballets and three divertissements I have done in 4 and a half months!! Performances are given every day, I am on the stage every evening, but when I leave, I shall not have 4,000 francs left after all the expenses I have to pay! M. Porto has passed this way but I do not know if he has been entrusted with forming the company.

Farewell, settle your matter with York, and believe me,

Yours ever,
A. Saint-Léon

10/2/55
Lisbon, 1 Largo San Carlos.

17

To G. B. Benelli

My dear Benelli,

I really believe I have not the gift of making myself understood by you. Is it my muddled style or my shapeless handwriting? You appear to be saying that I do not wish to pay you. That is steep! I have told you, and say again, that M. York claims that he has an arrangement under which you owe him half the fare, that you have acted in bad faith, and that you are the cause of his ruin because of the crowd of "cani" that you have made him engage (among whom is myself), and then finally he withholds a sum of 250 fr. and then another 250 fr. You can imagine that I have not given way in this without seeing M. York's proof and obtaining a copy of it, but you will also forgive me if I have not immediately complied with your demands. I have been to see your notary who does not wish to get involved in the affair, because your opponents are barely solvent and the lawyers much prefer it to be otherwise. But no matter, although you appear to mistrust me, I have perhaps done better than you

50

thought. I have summoned M. York by process-server to produce proof that you owe him half the fare. This summons has resulted in disclosing that M. York had no right and no document legally entitling him to this.

I have therefore demanded that the money M. York had retained, amounting to 500 fr., be paid to me. It is here that the difficulty lies, for a retention was indeed made but no cash was deposited! There have been recriminations and arguments, but it was all to no avail, because the administration is in a terrible condition and, it must be admitted, engagements have been made for the most part on a scale that would ruin Croesus. I have been promised I shall receive half tomorrow. You see, my dear Benelli, that before going to your lawyer, who has done nothing for you and who does not wish to do anything, I had done better on my own account than you were prepared to believe.

I am therefore sending you by tomorrow's post the sum of 375 francs, and when I get the rest I shall send it to you, that is I shall bring it to you. I have told you they were withholding 11⅛% because you had not put into the contract "francs in cash", and so there will be a deduction to make from the other quarter of your fees which seems to me more than reasonable. We can argue about that between ourselves, and I am sure there will be no blood spilt or disasters to lament. I hope we shall recoup all this through another engagement that you will arrange for me and in which there will be less bother, more money and above all francs in cash.

In anticipation I shake your hand and remain your devoted

A. Saint-Léon

18/3/55 Lisbon

Alboni will not be able to give all her performances. She still has 8 to give before the end of this month, but she is paid. As for me, I cannot say as much, I have already played . . .[1] 7 times!!!!!

To Leon Escudier[1]

My dear Escudier,

I hasten to reply to your letter of the 24th, which arrived here only yesterday. I have just arrived from Temesvar[2] where I gave a performance the day before yesterday, and already the Orchestra and the Ballet are waiting for me at the National Theatre for my two last performances.

The Lisbon proposals completely upset my plans. I am in the process of arranging a monster tour, but I jot down the conditions you request as they come to me. I cannot make any financial concessions to Lisbon, I had £120 sterling a month for the position of a galley slave and I stick to the same sum plus a benefit that I had before, without cost of travel – the right to revive some of my successful ballets such as *Saltarello*, *Lutin*, *Pâquerette*, and *Fleurs animées* – a condition that I need not stage more than 5 new ballets, large and small, in the whole season, nor dance two days in succession in grand ballets. So far as Fleury is concerned, I shall not enter into any agreement unless she is engaged jointly with me. Her salary must be £60 sterling a month and a benefit, as last year. As for Mlle. Pitteri[3], I will look after her as well as I have done for others. If a ballet includes two roles I shall use them both, otherwise one, and since Mlle. Pitteri will not know the old repertory I shall be able to give here more importance in the new works *without* however diminishing the position of an artist such as Mlle. Fleury.

If an arrangement is possible, please send me a list of the company, the second danseuses, the male dancer, who must also play comic parts as I did before, and the mimes etc. It goes without saying, of course, that I must be in charge of my company and be completely independent in everything relating to the composing of ballets.

I also want to know if the Government is in charge still, or a private management, which would complicate the situation dreadfully, and always in the event of agreement 5 or 6,000 francs advance is to be payable in Paris on 10th August, to be deducted by monthly instalments.

I finish here on Sunday and on Monday I am off to Dresden to stage the winter ballets for Mlle. Bose.[4] So send your reply as soon as possible to the Theatre Royal, Dresden, for on the 25th August I leave for Warsaw and Russia, Walachia, where things are almost settled or rather at my disposal.

In anticipation, believe me your devoted

A. Saint-Léon

Pesth, 1st July 1858

Also, let me know frankly your agency fee. We have had great successes in spite of the heat.

19

To Charles Formelle[1]

My dear Sir,

I would dearly like to exploit the theatres of Russia and Walachia with Mlle Fleury. By Russia I mean Moscow, Warsaw and Odessa, and by Walachia Bucarest, perhaps Jassy, which have excellent and well appointed theatres. I know that there is nothing to expect in Petersburg since Perrot rightly reigns there as absolute master and that in the other theatres they do not go to much expense. However, I have some effective works arranged for those kinds of establishment which require, so to speak, neither cost nor inconvenience, and I am almost certain that the result would be satisfactory. The combination of playing the violin on stage and dancing such as I introduce in *Le Violon du Diable*, *Le Dansomane*, *Le Lutin de la Vallée* always creates a sensation by its novely and originality. I have the music in orchestral parts and our costumes, and as for all else I find what is necessary in the theatres. I do not know what is the usual arrangement in these theatres; I do not think they give, as in Germany, half or a third of the receipts after deduction of expenses.

So if you could make arrangements with Moscow, Odessa and Warsaw, for us to give a dozen performances in each city, with a benefit, you would have cause to be very happy. Do you think that our fee should be 1,000 or 1,200 fr? You know Mlle Fleury, who is one of the most commendable of dancers.

20

To Emile Perrin[1]

To Monsieur Perrin, Director of the Académie Imp. etc.

Please forgive me, Monsieur le Directeur, if, though unknown to you, I take the liberty of writing this letter, but the engagement you have just made with Mlle Muravieva has naturally prompted me to do so.[2]

Almost 18 months ago H. E. Monsieur de Walewsky[3] allocated me one of his two next ballets at the Opéra. Last summer this promise was repeated on the part of the Minister, and M. Gautier of the Ministry of State told me that my turn would come after Mlle Taglioni's ballet.[4]

I do not think you have been informed of this promise, which was made before the direction was entrusted to you. I have letters to prove that I am only asking for what has been said, but at the same time I am not claiming to reopen these discussions if they are not convenient to you.

However, Muravieva has been entrusted to me since she became première danseuse and has made her rapid reputation in my works. She would, I believe, be very happy to find me on a foreign stage at an important moment of her career.

She has a ballet called *Météora* which suits her perfectly. Its subject is simple but practical and suitable to her personality. The production, without being costly, lends itself to some novel effects. If you wish to adapt it to accord with your taste, or change the title, while retaining Muravieva's principal situations, I guarantee a great dancing success. The music is one of the prettiest scores of Pugni and Pinto, and if the changes are not too great, the ballet would be ready in 15 days so far as I am concerned. The work is in two acts and 4 scenes. The last décor is the most important, the others can be arranged very well at little cost.[5]

Mlle Muravieva could send you a scenario so that you can decide everything you want to do with it. Permission to leave will be granted to me immediately if it is requested from Paris, for there is a general desire here that I should accompany Muravieva.

Now, Monsieur le Directeur, if you have made other arrangements which you cannot go back on, it only remains for me to ask you to forgive my approach in the hope that on another occasion you will remember me, whose only recommendation is the memory of my former successes at the Opéra and those that I have obtained during the past 10 years on the leading stages abroad.

Please accept, Monsieur le Directeur, my respectful wishes and believe me, your devoted

A.M. Saint-Léon

Maître de ballet of the Imperial Theatres of Russia

3 Goroshovaya Street, Russian Fire Insurance building,
St. Petersburg
20/2/1863 (Russian style)

P.S. If this proposal is in any way suitable, and to avoid delays in correspondence about fees, since I am not looking on this as a profit-making venture, whatever you decide will be accepted by me in advance and you may use this letter as necessary.

St. Léon

21

To H. Jürgens[1]

Dear Monsieur Jürgens,

I have the honour to report what has been agreed between M. Livoff and myself, outside my Petersburg engagement, regarding what I have received on account in Moscow and what remains owing to me.

For composing the ballet[2] in Moscow and getting there a month sooner than my contract with the Imperial Direction of Petersburg provided I asked that for the extra month I should be paid 1,200 roubles plus a half-benefit – the addition of travelling expenses and lodging remaining at my expense, nothing having been specified about this.

Copy of the account left with M. Livoff[3]

From 15th July to 15th August	1,200 R
From 15th August to 15th September after my engagement here[4]	833 –
From 15th October to 15th November	833 –
	2,866 –
received in Moscow	650 –
remaining due	2,216 –

In addition I have received my salary for the month

from 15th September to 15th October that I have worked here, which you were kind enough to pay me almost in advance when I found myself short. This is not shown above.

Please be assured of my high regard and believe me, dear Sir . . . (Undated and unsigned. Letter dates from November 1863 – I.G.)

22

To David fils of the Production Department of the Paris Opéra

My dear David,

I am a little late in replying to the proposals you were asked to make to me on behalf of M. Perrin, but forgive a poor devil who never leaves the rehearsal room and the theatre. Mme. Petipa's illness[1] and Bogdanova's refusal[2] to fulfil her obligations throw the whole burden on to Muravieva and the bother on to me. Finally to get down to business, this, in a nutshell, is what I am proposing: the six months are to be reduced to five, starting from 15th March, and the fee for these five months is to be unchanged at 10,000 fr. and my author's rights, because I shall be sacrificing a month in Moscow from 15th July to 15th August (Russian style) to oblige M. Perrin. This evening I took advantage of a moment of H.M. the Emperor's good humour[3] to make a request for leave to Count Borkh[4], who was present. It has been granted, but I need a definite word as soon as possible to get it ratified. My Moscow ballet[5] (arranged) comes out on the 6th at Muravieva's benefit. I have spent 21 days staging it, not to speak of the crushing duties and illness among my choreographic flock. Everything has been too hurried. Muravieva will dance a pas as a ghost (pretty-pretty). She is having enormous success. Give my regards to M. Perrin and if the thing can be arranged without upsetting the Director's plans too much, send me a sort of contract to conclude here unless a "yes" would be enough.

All best wishes to your father and to friends.

Your devoted

Saint-Léon

Sunday 26/1/64 (Russian style)
St. Petersburg

It has been agreed that I shall be engaged to stage *Le Dieu et la Bayadère,* a new ballet, and the divertissements in *L'Africaine* if the music for them is ready. However, in the event of the Direction not being in a position to have me compose this last divertissement, either because of the maestro's slowness or for any other reason other than my being at fault, my fees are not to be reduced.[6]

23

To Alexandre Mikhailovitch Borkh[1]

Your Excellency,

I have the honour to request your permission, as a very exceptional measure, for me to leave on the first day of Lent, when I shall have completed everything which the Imperial Direction has required of me.[2] I venture to hope that Monsieur le Comte will not refuse me this favour in view of the family and business circumstances that call me to Paris.

In anticipation I have the honour to remain Monsieur le Comte's humble servant,

A.M. Saint-Léon

20th February 1864
Petersburg

To Alexandre Mikhailovitch Borkh

Monsieur le Comte,

At the end of this season I shall complete the fifth year of my stay in Russia in the capacity of composer of ballets to the Imperial Theatres. During this time I have been happy to enrich the repertoire with seven ballets here and one in Moscow. Many times and even quite recently I have had the unique privilege of being honoured by His Majesty's approval of my works.

With you, Monsieur le Comte, I think I have always been punctual and willing to carry out orders, so please excuse me, Excellency, if at the moment of leaving for five months at the Paris Opéra, the cradle of my first successes, and my country, I come to beg you to kindly place before His Majesty the Emperor the request for a great favour, which for me would be the most precious and cherished of honours – the medal of one of His Majesty's orders.

In the hope that Monsieur le Comte will excuse any liberty I may have taken in making this approach, I have the honour to remain Your Excellency's very humble and obedient servant.

A. Saint-Léon
Maître de Ballet

Knight of the Order of Christ of Portugal
Holder of the Medal of Merit of Saxe-Coburg[1]

St. Petersburg
28/2/64

To H. Jürgens

Dear Sir,

Being, on the recommendation of H.E. Count Borkh, the object of an exceptional favour of His Majesty the Emperor, I have to acknowledge receipt of the gold watch and diploma which you have instructed M. Marcel to hand me on behalf of the Treasury of the Imperial Theatres.[1] I am adding to this letter my sincere thanks to you, dear Sir, who in all circumstances have never ceased to show me your benevolence, and beg you to accept the best wishes

with which I remain,
your devoted

A. Michel Saint-Léon

12th June 1864
Paris, 21 rue Laval

To Alexandre Mikhailovitch Borkh

Monsieur le Comte,

Through M. Marcel I received, on the 8th of this month, a letter from the Chief Accountant M. Jürgens accompanied by the gold medal and ribbon of the Imperial Order of St. Stanislas, informing me that, on your application, Monsieur le Comte, His Majesty has deigned to confer on me the insignia specified above.

In respectfully presenting my warm thanks to Monsieur le Comte I am only feebly expressing my most sincere gratitude, all the more since it is only most particularly to Monsieur le Comte's benevolence to me that I owe the great favour of which I have been the object. I venture to hope that Your Excellency will be good enough to convey to His Majesty the Emperor my most humble feelings of profound gratitude for the grace which He has deigned to bestow on me and which will remain forever engraved on my heart as the most treasured of my honours.

I have the honour to remain Monsieur le Comte's very devoted and grateful servant

A. Saint-Léon

Paris, 16th June 1864
21 rue Laval

27

To Emile Perrin

Monsieur le Directeur,

The letter you wrote to Count Borkh has had the desired effect. Yesterday evening, a few hours after receiving it, the Count gave me permission to leave as soon as *Herculanum*[1] is staged, which will enable me to be at your disposal between 25th and 29th January, new style.

Since you are overburdened with work, please do not trouble to write. For my part I shall advance the moment of my departure as much as possible, and as for my remuneration I leave to you, Monsieur le Directeur, as in the past, the task of fixing it at your convenience.

In anticipation of my departure I brought forward my benefit, which took place last Sunday with the 6th performance of *Koniok*[2] in the presence of His Majesty and all the Imperial family, and which brought in the maximum receipts at the prices for the Italians.[3]

Please receive my sincere respects and believe me,

Your devoted

M. Saint-Léon

St. Petersburg,
30th December/11th January 1865
79 Moika Canal, apt. 8.

To H. Jürgens

Dear Sir,

His Excellency Count Borkh, having considered the request made by the Imperial Direction in Paris, has informed me that I can leave after having attended the first perfce of *Herculanum*.[1] While waiting for the formal order of Count Borkh, I am writing to ask you to deliver my passports,[2] and those of Mme. Louise Fleury, so that they can be signed and ready and I shall not, on that account, suffer any further delay at the moment of leaving.

Relying on your kind cooperation, I have the honour to be, dear Sir,

Your very devoted

A. Michel Saint-Léon

Monday 11/1/65
Petersburg

To Emile Perrin

Monsieur le Directeur,

I have the honour to write to you from Moscow about the début of Mlle Grantzow[1], as you have asked me to do. Yesterday, November 15th, she danced *Fiammetta* for the 1st time. She had to contend with an impatient and severe public, and the memory of Muravieva and Lebedeva[2], the idol of the Muscovites; further, she was the first foreigner in 12 years to endeavour to overcome the obstacle of nationality. For my part, since I had instructions from Ct. Borkh to bring her back to Petersburg if she was badly received, I wanted to put her to the test with a single stroke and I did not have a ticket to spare in the whole theatre. The

Emile Perrin, Director of the Paris Opéra from 1862 to 1870.
(Bibl. de l'Opéra)

Charles Nuitter, Archivist of the Paris Opéra from 1866 to 1899.
(Bibl. de l'Opéra)

Marfa Muravieva in *Néméa* (1864). Photograph by Disdéri.
(Bibl. de l'Opéra)

UNE
RÉPÉTITION A L'OPÉRA
(NÉMÉA OU L'AMOUR VENGÉ)

Saint-Léon rehearsing *Néméa* (1864). From *La Vie Parisienne* of 16th July 1864. (Bibl. de l'Opéra)

poor girl was playing in a *ballet* for the 1st time; hitherto her repertoire had consisted only of the Nun in *Robert*[3], *Fenella*[4], and isolated pas. In spite of these handicaps and great nervousness she roused the public to enthusiasm as in the greatest days of her predecessors. In the interests of truth I must say that I have never seen a talent more complete, and so varied and excellent in every style. Her appearance in the evening is charming, and I thought of your words when I heard people say yesterday "She is like the young Elssler." Yes, but Elssler never had her suppleness or her ballon, and she has in addition amazing pointes, tacqueté, batterie, an expressiveness in her miming and her dancing worthy of a great artist, and a confidence as if she had played in grand ballets for 20 years. In the 4th act she was as light, delicate and vigorous as in the 1st.

Her most enthusiastic admirers accompanied her to her hotel, behind her carriage, applauding. 4 performances have been sold out from today, and to complete these antics the régisseur has recorded 33 curtain calls. Her success has therefore been complete. God knows what these crazy people are going to think up, but what has really touched me is to find such a rare intelligence and such a perfect talent.

If I were you, I would hurry and let Paris see her in all her freshness. She would be suitable to play in the whole of Muravieva's repertoire, which would entail no delay in the plans you might have. In spite of the penalty I made her pay in Hanover, she would come on Muravieva's terms for the 1st year and I can guarantee you a real and great success. She could dance from about 15th March to the end of July or August.

I will supervise her début with great pleasure and for nothing, but please let me have a reply as soon as possible or get someone to write to me if you are too busy, because I shall have to make another decision if my request is not timely.

I am reviving *Météora* for the continuation of her

début performances, and then return to Petersburg for Lebedeva, who injured herself during a rehearsal of *Pâquerette* three weeks ago. She too has had a great success in *Fiammetta*, but then she is Russian.[5]

Mme. Petipa is losing her strength from day to day, and my Russian ballet continues to make enormous receipts without a 1ere danseuse.[6]

Minkus, with whom I am living and working out a new ballet on a national legend, wishes to be remembered to you.[7]

L'Africaine is still in the air, but if it is given it will be interpreted in such a way to kill the work at a single blow.

Please reply as soon as possible, and accept my best wishes.

A.M. Saint-Léon

My usual address, whether I am in Moscow or not, is No. 1 Nicholas Street, Dom Fittingoff, apartment 18, by the Bolshoi Theatre, St. Petersburg. Letters addressed to the theatre take six to eight days to reach us.

Moscow, 16th November 1865
Russian style

30

To Madame Dominique

Moscow, 18th November 1865 R.St.

My dear Caroline,

On Monday the 15th Adèle made her début in *Fiammetta* and had an enormous success, being recalled 22 times during the evening in spite of memories of Muravieva and Lebedeva and the handicap of nationality, stronger here than in Petersburg. She was beyond all praise. This ballet, which is much more important than in Paris, found in her its true interpreter.

Naturally I have looked after this child as best I could, but she is worth the trouble. Her talent is *now at its most complete*, and its effect is not lost on the stage, on the contrary. I did not want to place a single claqueur in the house, for I had orders to bring her back to Petersburg if she suffered the slightest unpleasantness from prejudice. Before a full house, the largest in Europe, she electrified that damned crowd with enormous assurance. Encores, hastily purchased flowers in the last act, and escorted home with the most infatuated bravos. That is a good start. God knows where it will end. So here she is launched at a single bound, and a true prima ballerina in a country which may be the dirtiest but where the pay is really good. She has suffered from the climate, fleas, lice, bugs, the food, the air, but at least here she is in the saddle.

I am mad about her. Always having to deal with dancers whose mechanism has to be concealed, it is good to have a merry little girl who possesses *everything*. She is even pretty in the evening, is ready before everyone else, and has no (illegible), but that is a blessing.

The theatre is sold out three times over. I am already producing *Météora* for her, she is delightful in it. Afterwards I shall return to Petersburg for Lebedeva who has injured herself. I shall give *Pâquerette* there, then a new work for her benefit, and I shall return for Adèle and mount *Giselle* for her and *Les Noces Valaques* for her benefit, then a little ballet for the other one here.[1] Well to the hell with it, for I am up to the eyes. Now I have a favour to ask you, it is a question of seeing Cray – or Crai[2], it doesn't matter which – to order 4 dozen shoes, like the first ones – the last were too long – and send them as quickly as possible by Maillard's, 30 rue Bergère, addressed to the Administration of the Imperial Theatres in Moscow for Mlle Grantzow. The bill will be paid in Paris on my behalf at M. Laurent's, 21 rue Laval[3] – just let me know the amount – but for

God's sake see that the shoes are good and ready soon. She is to be reengaged here, on proper terms. I am working out a scheme and at all costs she will make her début in Paris – if not wanted at the Opéra, then elsewhere. The artistes have invited us to a supper after the 1ere. She is enjoying herself here and her health is better now. Don't forget my commission. Adèle sends you thousands and thousands and thousands of good wishes. Unfortunately she does not write French. So many thanks, Caroline, a large part of this success is due to you since it was you who made me see her. Thanks. Best wishes to Dominique, Louise Barratte, Beaugrand and my poor little invalid Ribet.[4]

I know that wonders are in preparation. All the better, I hope to be able to steal something. I am living at Minkus's, and we are preparing a grand Russian ballet for next year. My *Koniok* has grossed nearly 300,000 fr. and that without the ballerina. The one who dances it in Petersburg makes me sick, but she is protected by the Minister, damn it![5]

So long, Dominique, there are still 2 months 18 days 14 hours and 57 minutes to go before we meet again, and I hope to find you both hale and hearty.

Your devoted

A.M. Saint-Léon

Only 2 months 18 days and 54 minutes to go.

Don't forget Petit and his wife and Jeanneton, and the Monge family. Give my best regards to M. Cormon. I find they are not giving *Néméa* often enough.[6] What am I going to buy my cigars with? Reduced to Crapulados!! Oh. heavens!

31

To Emile Perrin

Monsieur le Directeur,

I have the honour to write to you from Moscow about Mlle. Grantzow, as you seem to wish, before my departure.

I know how busy you are, and would not have troubled you today if Mlle. Grantzow had not sent me a letter from M. Dejean of the Toffoli agency containing an offer for your theatre after the Moscow season. As I was the first to speak to you about this artist whose success is well deserved and very great, I suppose you did not have to get in touch with an agent which does not seem to be your usual custom.

On my return from Moscow she will sign a brilliant contract for Russia, but I have arranged it in such a way as to enable her to leave after the Italian seasons, that is at the end of Carnival.[1]

I am asking you, Monsieur le Directeur, to be so good as to let me have a line about this matter so that I know your plans. I would be sorry to arrange something else for this magnificent talent if you feel you should profit by it, but she does not want to have nothing to do after Moscow.

Today we had the general rehearsal of *L'Africaine*[2] without the "Africaine". Mlle Barbot[3] sent word at 7 o'clock that she was unable to sing. It was quite ridiculous, but such things can only happen here. The house was completely full, and the principal role was hummed by the conductor. The costumes for the ballet are bad parodies of the Paris ones. On 2nd January the revival of *Théolinde*[4] is being given for Mlle Lebedeva. Then I shall leave for Moscow again to produce *Giselle* and a short ballet for Mlle Grantzow's benefit. Her success in *Météora* has been greater than in *Fiammetta*.[5]

Mlle Bogdanova has written to tell M. Suvarov, Governor of St. Petersburg,[6] and Minister Adlerberg[7] that her success in Paris was enormous and that it would have been greater still if I had not run down her talent. However, I do not think I was far from the truth in describing her as unsuitable for a serious stage. Perhaps in Berlin she will triumph over the wrong I was able to do her in Paris.[8]

In the hope that you will kindly favour me with a reply, I beg you, Monsieur le Directeur, to accept my best wishes.

A.M. Saint-Léon

23/12/1865 (Russian style)
St. Petersburg
Dom Fittingoff, Apt. 10,
Bridge of Kisses, near the Italian Theatre

32

To Emile Perrin[1]

Monsieur le Directeur,

I have to thank you very warmly for your telegram and your letter of 9th January to which I have been unable to reply sooner because of the 1ère of *L'Africaine*, which took place yesterday, and the rehearsals for the revival of *Théolinde*, which we are giving on Sunday for Lebedeva's benefit.[2]

M. Toffoli has written to me again, but I do not know what to think of it now thanks to your kindness.

Mlle. Grantzow finishes on 19th February 1866, new style, and should be at your disposal from 15th March or 1st April until 15th September, n.s.

For her first début, *Néméa* or *Giselle*, as you choose.

She is also charming in *La Fille mal gardée*, which I made her study before my departure from Moscow. This ballet, refurbished with modern pas, would perhaps be a pleasing and not very expensive revival while waiting for the new work, if you are agreeable. I do not mention *Diavolina*, because Beaugrand plays it, but she is also very good in that. On Tuesday I shall be in Moscow to arrange her benefit, and I shall inform her of your courteous letter about her, and as for the reduction you wish, I thought of 1,500 fr. spread over the three months, i.e. 2,000 instead of 2,500. The expense of making one's début in Paris is very considerable.

As for her future I have made her sign up only for next season, for 6,000 R, 35 R performance bonus, benefit guaranteed at 2,000 R, 250 travel expenses. If her success matches up to her talent, you will be able to take such action as you wish. Above all it is, I believe, essential that she should make the impact of which she is capable. Only yesterday Count Borkh told me he had some people from Moscow in his box who claimed they could not look at the marvels of Petersburg after Grantzow. And in addition she fills the house every evening with the old ballets. Now she is in Moscow, and *Koniok* – given in Petersburg without a ballerina – enjoys the choreographic honours in both capitals.

L'Africaine, which is reasonably performed in the crowd scenes, has been received extremely coldly. With the help of the Grand Duke Constantine[3], I have got several of Mr. Costa's unworthy cuts restored. The ballet is the same as in Paris except (my God!) the women's costumes. You have really spoilt me, Monsieur le Directeur. I have paid dearly here for the pleasure that I got out of this at the Opéra.[4]

I do not know what will be the outcome of this masterpiece, which is a fine one in spite of being revoltingly mutilated, but it is extraordinary to give such a work 31 days before the end of the season.

I shall have the honour to write to you from Moscow

as soon as I have seen Grantzow, and I shall be grateful if you would make a decision on the Moscow letter. Renewing my sincere thanks, Monsieur le Directeur, I am, yours sincerely,

A.M. Saint-Léon

Petersburg 7/1/1866 Russian style

Letters sent to Petersburg with my interminable address do not arrive in Moscow.

33

To Emile Perrin

Monsieur le Directeur,

I have informed Mlle Grantzow of your kind letter which she appreciated very much. She begs you not to make too large a reduction, for she has a penalty to pay and she calculates that her début is going to cost her the earth. In your reply please make it clear that the variation is to relate only to the first 3 months. In this way she will be at your disposal from 1st or 15th April, as you wish, until 15th September, at 2,000 frs. for the first 3 months, and 2,500 frs for the last 2. I think *Néméa* will suit her better than *Giselle* for the 1st début, but you will make the choice at your discretion.

She is having an enormous success here. For her benefit she is to receive 7 presents valued at about 10,000 francs.

On the 30th, Russian style, I leave for St. Petersburg and you can give me a definite answer before the end of the season, 19th February, new style, my mission will be infinitely easier. Awaiting your reply, Monsieur le Directeur, please accept my best wishes and believe me, your very devoted

A.M. Saint-Léon

17/1 Russian style
Moscow

Grantzow danced *Météora* this evening to a packed house. From all accounts she was admirable in it.

If you present her in Paris, I am sure you will have cause for satisfaction. I have never seen this ballet so perfectly performed, even by Muravieva.

Please address letters to me at Petersburg

34

To Emile Perrin

Arrival No: 8446
Sent to home address, 5.45 p.m.
14th February 66

V. PRUSSIA, PARIS FROM PETERSBURG

104 20 14 1 32 S. PARIS PERRIN OPERA
CAN DEPART SATURDAY 8TH TELEGRAPH IF SUITABLE WILL REFUSE MOSCOW ENGAGEMENT TO HELP YOU. SAINT-LEON

35

To Alexandre Mikhailovitch Borkh

Monsieur le Comte,

The day before yesterday, 8th April, I received your letter of the 3rd instant in which you tell me that the specification for the production of *Koniok* in Moscow has been accepted. At the same time you ask me to settle with you the date of my return. This is laid down in my contract as 1st August if I am needed, or if not, the 15th. Consequently I am ready to return on one of these two dates as soon as you let me know which, *provided that I can rehearse with the company immediately on my arrival.* It would be better for me to start in Petersburg, where Mlle. Lebedeva is without a new work, and then to go to Moscow. I have used my stay in this latter city to prepare an act and a half of music with Minkus with your agreement.[1] That will speed up *Zolotaia Ribka* considerably.

I am sorry to be unable to meet your wishes regarding the costumes of this ballet. But it is *practicably impossible* to give designs in advance for an entirely new ballet.

This same question was raised at the time of *Koniok* and I was unable to accede to it then. This procedure is not customary in the theatre because it is not practicable. I can give, near enough, the number, which will be rather less than for *Koniok*, and I will do as I did for that ballet by detailing the costumes and the type, as well as the exact number, as soon as a scene has been set and arranged. In that way there is no duplication of work or confusion and the author does not fetter his ideas with doubtful orders.

You are probably aware of the decision that has just struck the Temple of Art in France. H.M. Napoleon, at the suggestion of Marshal Vaillant[2], has declared that the I. Theatre of the Opéra is no longer to be part of the Emperor's Household. He is increasing the subsidy to 900,000 francs and is to choose a Director to run it at his own risk and deposit 500,000 fr. as security.

The effect of this reorganisation is detestable, and since yesterday there has been talk of the City of Paris taking the whole thing over and choosing a Director.

The original cause of this disaster is the musicians of the orchestra who demanded and obtained an increase of salary but were not satisfied with it. Then, when a tenor took over *La Juive* at short notice, the public created a terrible uproar, even though a proper announcement had been made.[3] They sang the *Marseillaise* and hissed. M. Perrin, a man of integrity and undeniable talent, has many enemies among the abonnés, principally because he is very cold and dignified. These gentlemen do not have enough power in the theatre for their liking. As for me I would miss him, but I do not think he has left.[4]

The revival of *Don Juan* has created a great stir. Interpretation, décor, production form a superb ensemble.

The divertissement I was commissioned to interpolate in it, to music selected by myself from the symphonic works of the master, was a unanimous success both musically and choreographically.[5]

Mlle Grantzow arrives tomorrow and will make her début at the end of April when *Don Juan* comes off because of the holidays of Faure, Battu, Saxe and Mauduit.[6] I am working on a ballet in two acts and four scenes which will be given in June, provided the new administrative arrangements do not change these plans.[7] While waiting for her new ballet she will dance *Giselle*, *Néméa*. I shall have the honour to inform you of the result of her début.

At the Théâtre Italien I have also had a great success with *Les Noces Valaques*, a one-act ballet.[8]

I shall await a definite word from Your Excellency as to whether I am to begin my duties in the first days of August, and whether in Petersburg or Moscow. Hoping that you will not have forgotten my request, to which I shall be very happy to receive a response. I have the honour to remain Monsieur le Comte's very humble and obedient servant,

A.M. Saint-Léon

Paris
11th April 66
21 rue de Laval

36

To Alexandre Mikhailovitch Borkh

Monsieur le Comte,

I have already had the honour of informing Your Excellency that it is impossible for me to give the costume designs of the new ballet *Zolotaia Ribka*, explaining first how inconvenient it is to order things which at the moment of composition often become scenically impracticable, and then the demands that arise during the setting of the action and the consequent inhibition of the composer if work is done blind and simply to a set plan. These reasons have *always*, *everywhere* and *at all times* prevented authors from giving the costumes and properties of a new work *before* it has been arranged. To save time I will give the costumes act by act, as I did for *Koniok*, which suffered no delay. As for the approximate total, it will not exceed that of *Koniok*, quite the contrary.

In the 26 years I have been a *maître de ballet*[1] I have never been able to do otherwise for a new work, although the thing is quite different when it is a matter of an old ballet or one that has been already performed.

I am extremely sorry not to be able to oblige. Monsieur le Comte, but *order*, *economy* and the *good of the work* for which I am responsible impose this course on me in the general interest. As for the scenery it will not undergo any significant or onerous modification. The plan given will stand in its entirety. I will, however, get in touch with M. Roller[2] for the last scene.

The ballet I am now composing for Mlle Grantzow (who had a complete and real success in *Giselle* and *Néméa*) goes ahead with all speed.[3] Yet they will only begin work on the costumes when I have set the ballet *on the stage*, as also for *Don Juan* and *Les Abeilles* which I am also producing. Even the scenery is not finally decided upon until the work is produced. To do otherwise would lead me to decline all responsibility.

In repeating my sincere regrets to Your Excellency I have the honour to be, Monsieur le Comte, your very obedient and grateful servant,

A.M. Saint-Léon

15th June 1866
21 rue de Laval
Paris

Although I have already thanked you in a separate letter for your kindness in supporting my request to His Majesty the Emperor about the gold medal and ribbon of St. Anne[4], I am taking the liberty of repeating my most profound gratitude, with which I have the honour to remain your very humble servant,

A.M. Saint-Léon

M. Théodore, who receives a pension from Russia and is at present ballet-master at the Théâtre Lyrique, knows and loves Russia.[5] He also knows the customs and the *andamento* of the Imperial Theatres. He has staged revivals of ballets by Perrot and others in Moscow, perfectly, and I consider him suitable to fill the post of *reproducer* of Petersburg ballets. He will be prepared to accept this post on these terms – 2,400 roubles and a half-benefit – available 1st August – his expenses paid for a combined railway and sea journey. He is also known in Moscow and gave honourable service there. The reason for his dismissal was that his daughter and his wife were dancers whom M. Saburov did not wish to retain. Now his daughter is abroad with her mother, and the father can act more independently. M. Gredelue is unable to accept the post since he wishes to have his wife engaged as 1ère danseuse and she is not very talented.[6]

If you wish to find out more about M. Théodore and then give me a reply, I can negotiate the matter so as to save you the cost of an agent.

In this way the Direction can arrange for him to prepare a ballet for Moscow that has been a success in Petersburg, and with the choreographer giving the finishing touch the matter can proceed quickly and exactly.

Once again I have the honour to send Monsieur le Comte my respects.

A.M. Saint-Léon

37

To Charles Nuitter

I am impatiently waiting, my dear Nuitter, for the moment when I can thank you for your good and affectionate letters. You are promptness itself, kindness in person. At last, thank God, I am getting better, but I am extremely weak and I get dizzy when I wish to read or write. It was in Berlin that I noticed the first symptoms of this wretched illness. I attribute this malady to the disappointment of abandoning our child[1] and I thought that the journey would overcome this indisposition, but I was wrong. The nearer I got to my destination, the worse I became, and I only just had time to find a bed in which I have lain for 14 full days. I have to remain in my room for another week if nothing new develops. When I saw myself confined to my bed I lost all hope of arranging something to the advantage of our *Source.* Also, I have just learnt that Petipa is to revive *Le Diable amoureux* while I am staging *Koniok* in Moscow.[2] On my return there is talk of festivities for the Betrothal[3] and my new ballet.[4] All that leads me very far from the point! And M. Perrin needs a production. Since everything is against us, there remains only M. Perrin's good taste to preside over the staging, your watchful eye over everything, and perhaps a little of my lucky star. Ask me anything you want. I will try and be as clear as possible.

Minkus has written to me and wishes M. Cadeau, with whom he has a special understanding, to represent him. As for the tempi[5] of everything I place myself entirely in the hands of my nervous collaborator and friend Delibes *who will not let anything flag*. If necessary, Minkus can write a letter to M. Perrin relating to M. Cadeau. Write to me in detail about the rehearsals. If Grantzow is still in Paris, tell her that in eight or ten days I shall be in Moscow, where she is expected.

If the Minister's cossack programme is changed, I shall take advantage of the smallest favourable incident to ask for 15 days leave. Unfortunately the ballets are played and used so much here and in Moscow that I find it difficult to see that this favour will be granted to me. Then there is this wretched marriage, and finally the evil eye has certainly been mixed up in it.

Many fond wishes on my part to all the principal interpreters of *La Source*, not forgetting Mathieu and Pluque[6] to whom I entrust the ensembles – the ending of the Pas des fusils perhaps, which is always finished too far back and without precision[7] – where are the shields? I will recommend to Mlle Salvioni and Delibes a *tacté* variation, to a violin solo, if she does not dance that of the 2nd act in the Mayseder style.[8] I could even send a sketch.

Oh, this cursed malady and this damned war, a fatal combination, wretched circumstances that prevent me from entering port[9]. I cried "land" too soon. Please pay my respects to M. Perrin (together with a long sigh). If you only knew how tormented I have been during my illness! In my delirium I seemed to be for ever rehearsing.

Write to me often and much. Many compliments to everyone, not forgetting your father. But enough, I am getting dizzy, my eyes are giving me trouble, and anger is making me sweat, just as I used to do after a pas de deux! I must stop.

Your affectionate and devoted

A.M. Saint-Léon

Psbg.
30th August R.St.
1866

Always send letters to that happy Bridge of Kisses. If you only knew how bored I am there!!!!!!!!!!!!!!

38

To Charles Nuitter

Dear Nuitter,

It was an evening of emotions yesterday, the 21st. First, I received a telegram from M. Perrin, dated the 19th from Paris (what has caused this delay?). The leave that the Director requested for me in that dispatch was naturally refused by Borkh this morning. It was only to be expected. I arrived 13 days late, then came my illness, with the result that I have so far done nothing. I am stuck here and in Moscow until the end of November (Russian), and consequently we cannot think any more about it, profoundly sorry though I am! A few moments after the telegram I received your letter – another shock. This morning I rehearsed on the stage *Fiammetta* and the 4th act of *L'Africaine* for the Gala on the 16th,[1] and I designed the lance and the hook which you will find enclosed with a few notes. Also, Minkus sends me 3 measures to interpolate after the Waltz of death, 4th scene, which ends in E flat.[2] These 3 measures will be a better transition to the motif in G, 4 bars, which follows. Delibes pointed this out to me, and

78

Saint-Léon in rehearsal. Anonymous caricature.
(Archives Nationales)

Ludwig Minkus. Photograph by B. Braquehais. (Bibl. Nationale)

Madame Dominique in 1864. Photograph by S. Bureau.
(Collection of Ivor Guest)

A page from Saint-Léon's *répétiteur* score of *Il Basilico* (1865) "with scenistenochoreographic details." (Bibl. de l'Opéra)

Minkus asks either M. Cadeau or Delibes to orchestrate them.

With regard to all you tell me I have only one thing on which I insist as essential. It is my gliding group of the 4th act. This group, having been done only once, is disparaged as being ineffective. It is not easy to think of anything novel, so if Mlle. Salvioni cannot reproduce it as it was, I beg her to replace it at once *entirely*. At least I can make use of it another time. What impression does she make as a dancer? The idea of putting a veil on the little Mayfly to represent the cocoon might be a good one. I also want there to be a ray of sunshine at the moment of its birth, but at the beginning of the ballet try and get a half-light, not full light. Try out the shields with the new hooks. It would be a simple matter, if that does not please, to put the Source on to a palanquin. That would not change anything, but I looked over this march again the other evening and it is original.

You know I am in agreement for the royalties to be divided in quarters. Can you look after the sale of Minkus's author's tickets as advantageously as possible.

What should I do with mine? Must I give them to David?

Finally, keep your spirits up, my dear friend, and be happy if it is a success. On Monday I begin my new ballet[3] while an intelligent régisseur[4] is going to descend on Moscow to do 4 scenes from *Koniok*, which I shall then complete.

Grantzow is late, she was expected to arrive today. Mlle Salvioni is making moves to be engaged in Russia.

Our ballet is sick, our danseuses are even more so. Except for two young ones who have beauty and the devil's own talent, it is enough to give one dance-ophobia. Lebedeva[5] is going to kill my new ballet, which I am beginning without any enthusiasm. Until the ballet[6] is given, keep me in touch with everything, make this sacrifice for me. You will understand my anxiety.

If M. Perrin does not speak to you about the telegram, say nothing to him. I will write to him in the next few days, but I replied this morning by telegram. There must have been some interruption for the dispatch had on it "with Posto de Galen". What comforts me on one side is that I am not at fault for what has happened. My health is improving slowly, but my stomach is still weak and out of order. Farewell, my dear friend, excuse this indecent scribble.

Best wishes to everyone.

Your devoted

Saint-Léon

Psbg. 10th Sept. (R.St.), evening

39

To Charles Nuitter

TELEGRAM

From Petersburg
Received at 3.26 p.m.

Office: Place de la Bourse
Arrival No.: 25173
Sent to home address,
6 p.m. 6.10.1866

PARIS NUITTER RUE DROUOT
MINKUS AND MY BALLET SENT TO DAVID
FOR SALE OF MUSIC WRITE TO DELIBES
SAINT LEON

40

To Charles Nuitter

My dear Nuitter,

Having reread your titles for the dances I ask if the omission of the Pas du Hamac[1] before that of the Guzla is intentional – I certainly do not like the name Pas de fusil. Finale would be preferable – the rifle plays a very minor part in it.[2] For the pas at the end put scène or pas de la talisman if you think of nothing else that relates to the Source's sacrifice or death. The rest is perfect. The names appear very good to me, but I thought that in this case the fairy creature should not be *baptised*. The Sylphide had no name other than the title. But you are in charge and whatever you do will be *ben fatto*. I shall bow and say *slousche*.[3]

Don't let Graziani have a seizure, but your scenario for *Les Noces* is at Tsarskoe Selo in the hands of the Imperial family.[4] There is talk of staging this little ballet at the gala for Dagmar's wedding on 26th Oct. (Russian), with Mme. Petipa.

If they want to rush into this new expense, for I shall produce it in great splendour and with an enormous cast, I shall let you know. I have estimated for 25,000 fr, 8 premières danseuses and 24 2nds to dance the ensembles with all the premiers danseurs and mimes. What a wedding it will be, but nothing is decided yet. The purse strings are kept terribly tight, the presents are small, the jewels have flaws or are dubious!!

I am making progress with my ballet. An act and a half is finished. Now I am going to come to a forced halt, both here because of *Le Diable amoureux* revived by Petipa and in Moscow because of Grantzow's illness. We are out of luck, including Minkus. The poor girl caught a chill and has quinsy. Minkus *prostoudilse toje*, which means he has a cold too, and I myself am on my 3rd cold *toje*, but I go out just the same. It froze this morning although the weather is fine. It is the wind that is awful.

Last Monday we thought that *La Source* was being given, as we were working on the new ballet at Minkus's. From time to time we stopped and paced up and down. The Siberian authors were obviously anxious. We went home at 2.10 in the morning – it was then midnight in Paris. All that was premature. Mlle. Salvioni must let her foot get better again – she has one that seems to give her trouble at times. A break after the première would, as you say, be very unfortunate.

I was very surprised and upset at the second false movement of the branch. It seemed so firm at Richer.[5] The papers I read are all very secretive about *La Source*. I have no news of Mlle Montaubry.[6] I would be grateful to have news of her, for she had a bad eye when I left. Looking forward to hearing from you, believe me your devoted

Saint-Léon

1st/13th October, Psbg.
Best wishes to my beautiful Nouredda, my superb gipsy, Beaugrand, Baratte, Sanlaville and tutti quanti.[7] All the best to Delibes, and from Minkus. Ask David from me to give M. Laurent, Mlle. Fleury's father, 21 rue de Laval, a ticket for the première. As for the stage hands I would give them 100 fr. I will send you a bill drawn on my notary to get this sum and pay it to them. For the lamp men, gas men and sweepers 50 fr. Do me the favour of telling them they will lose nothing by my absence. Be good enough too to hand the enclosed note to M. Challant, the dancer in the corps de ballet.

82

41

To Charles Nuitter

My dear Nuitter,

I am hurriedly writing to you to announce that *La Fiancée Valaque* will be performed at the Gala on 1st or 3rd November, Russian style, at the Hermitage Theatre in the Winter Palace which has not been used for 10 years. As it is customary to present the scenario of the new ballet to H.M. the Empress,[1] who has accepted it, you have time to send it to me if you wish to prepare one *ad hoc*. I am working night and day. Everything else is going well. Mme. Petipa plays the role of the Fiancée. The corps de ballet consists of eight 1ères danseuses from here and 24 2ndes danseuses, and the same number of men – peasants, servants – splendid costumes. But more antics awaited me for the Gala of the 28th at the Bolshoi Theatre. H.M. the Empress has chosen the 4th act of *L'Africaine*, and now she wants two acts or an abridgement of the first two acts of my new ballet, *without an interval* and lasting 50 minutes. What do you think of that? It is almost as rich as the fable of my decoration and above all my pension, but unfortunately it is a *cruel* joke.

Keep me informed about what M. Perrin decides for *La Source*, for in all probability I shall have an opportunity, in all these Galas (particularly the one in Moscow, which I am directing also), to arrange the Grantzow matter in favourable circumstances. The idea of *La Fille mal gardée* with a new ballerina is a good one but will have to wait. I do not have time to write to Graziani[2], so please do it for me, he lives at 16 rue de Berlin. I am up to the eyes, and Petipa too. This evening he rehearsed *Le Diable amoureux*, and yesterday the two of us had 4 rehearsals! I alone wielded the baton for 7 hours.[3] Oh pension, where are you!! I have confidence in M. Perrin, and I am sure that good taste will watch over the changes in the 2nd act. Happily I have finished at Tsarskoe Selo. There is no more dancing, and now they are getting ready for the confirmation and the official betrothal ceremony. I am not put out by this circumstance, which allows me to rest in my bed.

Please give my regards to M. Perrin and believe me, yours affectionately

Saint-Léon

Tuesday 11th October R.St.
Psbg.

42

To Charles Nuitter

My dear Nuitter,

I have not been able to answer your letter sooner. For the last eight days I have not taken off my black suit. I am at Tsarskoe Selo to arrange, en famille, dances for La Dagmar, and in the mornings I rehearse the new ballet here. That has not prevented me from thinking seriously about your *two questions*. The solution is not easy.

Clearly, if Mlle Salvioni's foot does not allow us to be sure of a series of performances, it would be simpler to make *La Source* the ballet for the Exhibition[1]. Frankly I think the ballet could only gain by that, and would come at a splendid moment.

The season here ends on 28th February (Russian style). Grantzow can be in Paris a week later. As for me, I think I shall be free at the end of December (Russian style) at the earliest, but I cannot dance *La Source*. Should all that not be enough, Grantzow must be got off the hook in January. In any case I cannot guarantee anything. It is clear that with a little goodwill, the Direction would lose nothing by that. *Koniok*, which is awaited in Moscow like the Messiah, can do without a good dancer, particularly at this time – it remains to be seen if they will see reason. Is it possible to have Fioretti[2] *at that time*? Where is she? For the time being I cannot ask for anything. Grantzow arrived 10 days late and then caught a real Moscow cold. She will not be dancing for 15 or 20 days.

I would have liked to give you more positive answers, but how? However, write and tell me what is being done, and, believe me, I am very sorry about the difficulties that M. Perrin is having. Happily, I am not to blame. Let us comfort ourselves that all is for the best, etc. etc. like the awful roasts I eat at the Palace. To think there is no *spit* or *roasting apparatus* at Tsarskoe, and what butter, what beds, and if you only knew how much all that costs the excellent Emperor, for he is really a good man. During all these days he has been distressingly sad. His ministers are in favour of hanging that gang of assassins, and he does not want to. To cut a long story short, at 4 o'clock on Monday morning I heard the bell of the Imperial chapel. Everybody got up. The chapel was shut. The Emperor was in it alone. A requiem mass was being sung on his orders. The execution of the man who led it all was to take place at 7 o'clock. At a quarter to five the telegraph went into action, 5 couriers left at full gallop, and he reprieved the condemned man from the death sentence and halved the terms of imprisonment of the others. Ever since then he has been happy, and this evening he danced the quadrille with his youngest daughter vis-à-vis the betrothed couple.[3]

Your scenario,[4] written by you in that beautiful Nuitterian script, was on H.M. the Empress's piano together with two anthems that are to be played at the banquet tomorrow. Tomorrow I shall have the reply so long as they have nothing else to do. Your début in Russia will be stylish but not warm. A gala performance! Oh, what a life! Where are you, David?

Minkus has left me, he went to Moscow this morning. The music for the 2nd Act is ready. Three more scenes to do!!

So far the ballet[5] goes well.

A thousand cose a tutti, and best wishes from Madame Minkus and your friend.

Saint-Léon

Tsarskoe Selo, 18th October, evening

<h2 style="text-align:center">43</h2>

To Charles Nuitter

My dear Nuitter,

I have received your letter in which you tell me you have sent the manuscript. Many, many thanks. What now, a fire in a dancer's dressingroom, what a disaster might have happened![1] Happily the *pajarniks* did their duty. Talking of *pajarniks* (firemen), I saw some of them arrested in an empty street near where I live, when they were returning from a fire. What attracted my attention was seeing them all undressing in front of a man I took to be their chief. Not at all, it was the Minister or rather Chief of Police who wanted to prove to their captain who was present that his men were nothing but thieves. He found things in the water carts, and their pockets, boots and helmets were full of knick-knacks. What a lovely story for a ballet. Their captain was dismissed. I am sorry because he was an enthusiastic clapper and one of our most faithful abonnés.

This morning I rehearsed with orchestra and scenery, first *La Fiancée*, then 51 minutes of the ballet *Zolotaia*. You know that H.M. the Empress asked me for 50 minutes of ballet. I have 51 minutes, and hope I shall not go to Simbirsk[2] for that. Everything went as if it were on wheels, particularly *La Fiancée,* in which there are no stage effects. Mme. Petipa is very good in it as danseuse plastique but as for technique – *nitchevo*. For three days I have been struggling with the uniform they want to rig me up in. I am the spit image of Crépeau, the court usher. Impossible to make any conquests. It is true that I have given up a lot of that. If you go ahead, good luck, for my part I assure you I will not be against it. The corps de ballet is admirable in *Les Noces*. They carry the end and the middle. I have stuffed it with the best and a great crowd of others.

We shall have the Prince Royal of Denmark, Prince Royal of Russia, Prince Royal of England,[3] all the Archdukes and Duchesses, and a host of minor sovereigns who are more or less without thrones.

Not yet au revoir, but meanwhile,

Yours ever,

A. M. Saint-Léon

4th November, French style, 1866
Psbg.

I will think of doing some research for your work when I have a little more free time but not before my return from Moscow.

44

To Charles Nuitter

My dear friend,

I am very late in thanking you for your friendship and promptness. Letters, telegrams, programmes, books and all that amid the chaos of a première, is more than kindness, it is devotion.[1] I am very grateful to you, and want to prove it.

On Monday evening, the day of the 1ère of *La Source*, I was at the famous bi-monthly dinner of the *faux-col*, and I did not think that the ballet would really be given.

At least it is not a mess. After the 1ère there is always a fortnight of stupidities, all ballets have them, but little by little they settle down and what good there is in them is appreciated. I am afraid of the press. Minkus and I are not on friendly terms. Happily the public is there. I shall remember the overwork for *Diavolina* for the rest of my life.[2] Ouch!!! I have not been able to write to you this week because the galas have been postponed. The Orthodox Princess[3] has influenza. This delay has caused me terrible embarrassment. I am forced to upset everything that has been done and to continue my ballet. *La Fiancée valaque* is to be expanded by 2 pas, and the corps de ballet, composed entirely of soloists (for the Court), has resumed its usual expression. I have no music and no ideas, and have to work at a terrible pressure.

How I loathe my profession. Just now I received your letter of Tuesday, I have read it several times and briefly it seems we have had a success. It is good that the last scene was successful.

The cool reception at the 1ère was to be expected in view of the change of ballerina.[4] The middle and the ending crown the work, and all goes well. I shall write to M. Perrin from here shortly, but meanwhile please thank him sincerely from me. I hope the box office is doing well. It is important, as you rightly say. My dear friend, let us hope. In Paris success is not decided immediately. The word must get around. Please give my thanks to Mlles. Salvioni, Fiocre, Beaugrand, Barratte, Sanlaville, MM. Mérante, Coralli, Dauty, Cornet, and my beautiful gypsy girl, and then to MM. Sacré, Hainl, Despléchin, Mathieu, Pluque, Lormier, Albert, and if you remember, MM. Petipa and Berthier.[5]

I ask you to let me have 4 playbills, small size, two of the 1ère, two of the 2nd, I have a collection of my own.

I only received your two scenarios today. Another time, I forgot to tell you, send everything to the Administration of the Theatres. I have shown them to the Minister, who was present at the revision of *La Fiancée*. Your caligraphy arouses everyone's admiration. The binding is superb. We will settle up between us in Paris. The playbills are ready, and we now wait. Here is your name in Russian – Нюиттер . I shall keep a playbill and a printed programme of the gala for you.

I telegraphed Minkus on Wednesday at midday. Your telegram arrived at 5 o'clock in the morning. What a pity I still have to wait so long before seeing you all again. However, people have been sledging since yesterday, and there is a lot of snow. 10° at this moment, it is the beginning of the end.

For the moment I do not foresee any possibility of my returning before January (Russian). This year is exceptional.

I await news of Delibes. If he forgets me completely, I shall be angry with him, but in the meantime give him my congratulations, as the Russians say, and in a few days' time we shall be mutually congratulating one another if the receipts are good and the success keeps up and grows.

My scribble is indecent, forgive me, but I have so much to do and my health is certainly not brilliant – abominable headaches, rheumatic pains, bad stomach, and I am no longer 18!!!

As for you, my dear Nuitter, I am at a loss for words to thank you as I would wish. I shall certainly never forget what you have done for me on this occasion. Best wishes to your father. Thanks, thanks.

Your affectionate

A. Saint-Léon

Saturday evening
Pbg.

The lady who brought me up lives at 30 rue N^e Coquenard. If you have a box in the 4th tier one of these days, M. Lormier will ask you to give it to Mme Aglaé Gillet. Do not forget my thanks to David as well.

To Charles Nuitter

Dear friend,

A great success this evening.[1] The first part of my ballet *Zolotaia* went off perfectly, congratulations from the Emperor and all the Grand Dukes, and prophesies of a brilliant result (if I continue!) The house was superb. They played the three national anthems, Russian, English and Danish, and the unison chorus from *L'Africaine*, then the 4th act of the same opera, and after that my ballet. Minkus's music was successful. Dances, scenery, effects, nothing went wrong. Length 48 minutes. Now for Friday evening. On Saturday I leave for Moscow for *Koniok*. Before my departure and immediately after the performance I shall telegraph you. But here I am, alas, seriously shackled. I have to work like a packhorse. Ma poco denaro. It seems from what you tell me that the 2nd performance went off well. Let us wait and see. The *Indépendance Belge* also speaks well. But as regards myself it refrains from praise. Were the dances not successful? Bother that critic. Keep a few articles please, I am recovering my spirits now that I have almost 2 acts ready. Whew!

I stop for this evening, I am somewhat worn out.

Yours ever,

Saint-Léon

Tuesday evening
8th November
Psbg.

My thanks to your father

From 26th November, new style, at Moscow, Hôtel de Paris, chez Morel, Gd. Petrofka.

To Charles Nuitter

Friday evening, or
rather, Saturday
morning

11th Nov (R. St.)

Dear Nuitter,

I have just come from the gala performance at the Hermitage.[1] H.M. the Emperor was pleased, and H.M. the Empress conveyed to me, through the Grand Duke Nicholas,[2] that on this occasion she had no objection to the ballet and that it was charming. I had all the dancers dressed almost to the ankles so that she would have nothing to say. So *La Fiancée* is launched. As I am leaving at 2.30 for Moscow *La Fiancée* will be given twice unchanged. Then on my return 2 pas will be added to the ballet. One is already done. Your manuscript has been handed to H.M. Empress, but the Emperor had already looked at it the day before the rehearsal. I gave you a plug. He asked me if you were a ballet-master or a dancer. That is what comes of mixing with people beneath your station.

Well, everything is for the best. Complete success at the two galas.

If you write to me in Moscow, the address is just Hotel Morel, Grande Petrofka.

Le Nord, Léa in the *Journal de Pétersbourg*[3] and *L'Indépendance* are luke-warm about the ballet, but clearly they cannot deny it has been a success.

I am up to my eyes. I have had too much, but must carry on. The King and all the Princes and foreign ambassadors filled the front rows behind the Imperial family. The auditorium is like an amphitheatre with the benches forming a semicircle, in crimson velvet, all the ladies on one side and all the decorations etc. on the other, and at the back the enormous halls of the Winter Garden – a splendid effect, particularly if you look through the window where the frozen Neva gives you the shivers. I had to preside at the supper for my ballet company, 60 places allotted to the ballet, 25 champagnes and 40 Bordeaux (sic), with St. Léon transformed into a head waiter. After 5 toasts, naturally proposed by me to their Majesties and the bridal couple, I called for the carriages and *gattova*[4]. The music was much appreciated and the Emperor applauded each verse of the *Tresse d'or* [5]. H.M. the Empress gave the signal for the applause after "La Mélancholie" and the blessing of the golden threads. Perfect execution by the corps de ballet, which was made up of all the first, second and third dancers, Mme. Petipa was pretty, but I missed Urban.[6] On Sunday, God willing, I shall see Minkus and Grantzow. I shall soothe the despair of the former, who has been very badly and unjustly treated by Léa,★ gets worked up too, but at least he is mentioned, while in none of the 3 articles, including the *Débats*, have I come across my name. No one is . . .[7] even if there are any prophets. So long as the ballet is liked, *bolsche nitschevo*. Au revoir, and if you can give me news now and again, although I make use of you, you will give me great pleasure.

Yours ever,

Saint-Léon

★*Journal de Pétersbourg*

47

To Alexandre Mikhailovitch Borkh

Monsieur le Comte,

Honestly I must say that I certainly did not expect to receive the notice that M. Palt read to me on your behalf the day before yesterday, the 22nd instant.

How can the Direction deny me a legal right, due under contract, in a season when I am giving more than ever undeniable proof of exceptional toil?

Am I to be the dupe of the *Imperial* Theatres for having sacrificed my temporary interests last year, and given as much help as I could in fulfilling your benefit obligations to the artistes of Petersburg and Moscow? The Imperial Direction has appreciated this so much that it has not even *been able to notify me of the day of my benefit.*[1]

Is there a reason why I should lose it?

Have I caused such offence in my own interest through having full confidence in the Direction, when these benefits form part of my emoluments, which have already been so much reduced by the rate of exchange?

Did not Monsieur le Comte honour me last summer by expressing his entire satisfaction and that of the Imperial Direction?

And quite recently Monsieur le Comte in no way opposed what had been verbally agreed about the renewal of my engagement if *Koniok* was given in Moscow.

Indeed that would be more natural, since I was staging a ballet in Moscow and a ballet in Petersburg, than to give the benefit that is overdue in Moscow, and the other, for this year, in Petersburg?

Perrot, Bogdanov, Frédéric and Petipa all had benefits here when they staged works, most of them by grace and favour.

For what purpose will I have proposed sending M.

Bogdanov[2] and paying him 200 roubles to hasten the production of this important work, which will be staged in six weeks? Monsieur le Comte must see that I have been taken advantage of, for the galas would have prevented the production of one ballet or the other.

Truly, Monsieur le Comte, I do not understand it. After eight years of conscientious and happy work, I did not expect this.

I have always been sincerely devoted to the Imperial Direction. I was delighted by the successes I obtained under the superintendance of Monsieur le Comte, and I am distressed to think that this order emanates spontaneously from Your Excellency's loyal and honourable character.

I am hurt and discouraged, but I shall fulfil my duties *here* to the end. Only allow me, Monsieur le Comte, to protest here and now. Since last year's benefit has not taken place, not through my fault (as I am in a position to prove), the Imperial Direction owes me *either compensation or my benefit*, otherwise it will be in breach of one of the clauses of last year's contract, an eventuality provided for in the engagement.[3]

Please accept, Monsieur le Comte, the assurance of my esteem and believe me, your obedient servant,

A. Michel Saint-Léon

24th November
Moscow

Guglielmina Salvioni. (Collection of Ivor Guest)

Saint-Léon's instructions for the lances used in *La Source*.
See Letter 38. (Archives Nationales)

Praskovia Lebedeva. Photograph by Levitsky. (Bibl. Nationale)

Imp. A. Salmon, Paris.

Adèle Grantzow. Portrait by Léon Flameng. (Bibl. de l'Opéra)

48

To Charles Nuitter

My dear Nuitter,

For a change I am rehearsing 7 and eight hours a day. I have had a big rehearsal[1] today, and tomorrow is the first general rehearsal. I think I shall enter port on Wednesday or Thursday. The ballet is well staged, and Moscow certainly possesses the finest corps de ballet in the world. In 11 days I have set on the stage 4 *crowd* scenes of *Koniok* – it is incredible, I assure you – and it goes briskly. But also what a corps de ballet! How intelligent it is, and what style! Grantzow will be very good in it. This morning, seeing Grantzow dancing the famous elegiac mazurka[2] and Minkus playing the solo, I thought of you and our *Source* in Paris. In spite of that I prefer Moscow to Petersburg, and very much. First of all, I am in my element here. People adore the ballet, which dominates the repertoire. Apart from Grantzow, there is another very good première, who is particularly intelligent[3], a score of young second danseuses, male dancers (and male dancers are still applauded here), an orchestra whom I treat as I like, 2 excellent ballet conductors, and all *slousche, slousche*[4] with arms shouldered. And they *dance the pas slaves – my mania, as you know – wonderfully*. Then in Moscow there is real milk, real butter, cigars – ahh!!!! what cigars – and real artists and good fellows such as Rubinstein, Wienansky, Door, Honoré, pianists, and the famous quartet Laub, Cossman, Cserny and Minkus[5].

Apparently Delibes has not sold the music. The ballet is positively out of favour in Paris.

In eight or ten days I shall be in Petersburg again to finish *Le Poisson doré*. Another excitement – I have received two letters from you. I shall not thank you any more. I have carried out your orders, and Madame, friend Minkus and Grantzow send you thousands of good wishes.

My dear friend, I have rehearsed from 11 o'clock until 5.30 with more than 200 persons, and to finish it, from 7.30 to 9. I am now overcome by sleep, so excuse me.

Best wishes to everyone and be good enough to thank L. Marquet for her letter. I will answer her from Petersburg.

Au revoir, my dear friend, far away, down to my left it is December. Hum!

Looking forward to hearing from you,
Always yours affectionately,

A. M. Saint-Léon

Moscow
25th November 1866
Hôtel Morel, Grande Petrofka

I was woken up by a telegram from M. Perrin asking for me on 25th December. I have telegraphed him that I will give a definite answer in 10 days' time. For the first time I am having a little argument with the Direction. If they do not do right by me, I shall hand in my resignation – immediately on my arrival in Petersburg. If the matter is settled I shall be able to be in Paris before 20th or 25th January, and therefore too late for *Don Carlos*.[6] I have always been very loyal to the Direction but I will not stand for any injustice on its part.

Yours ever,

St. Léon

49

To Charles Nuitter

My dear Nuitter,

I am leaving Moscow tomorrow at the same time as this letter, with the difference that this will reach you in 5 days and your servant is going to resume his worthy career in Petersburg. The première of *Koniok* took place yesterday. A great success. Grantzow received 11,700 fr. for her share, so the takings totalled 23,400 fr. Nothing was lacking in this colossal ballet which I staged in 18 days!!!! I shall at least end up with the habit of making ballets.

Grantzow is going to Petersburg to dance there for 3 weeks. Her understudy[1] will play the role here, a strange and stupid arrangement. God willing, I shall be in Petersburg on Sunday morning if I do not freeze en route, for today we had 17 degrees Réaumur. I shall then see the Count[2]. I have a little quarrel with the Direction, and if I am crossed *I shall quit everything* and leave at once for *Carlos*, otherwise – and this is the trouble – I doubt whether I shall arrive in time.[3] Nevertheless I shall busy myself with the project I received from you yesterday.[4] I shall think of it on my way to Psbg. If I settle things with the Direction my ballet *Le Poisson* will be given in spite of Grantzow in the first days of the Russian January. This time I shall be free, but one should not count one's chickens before they are hatched. Shall I arrive in time – *that is the question*. "Saint-Léon for ever" would be a misnomer this time. I know that Verdi is very zealous and expeditious. I still have to know how things stand at the Opéra, the staging etc.

In any event I shall send a telegram to M. Perrin. Minkus drives me to despair, he is very lazy, he no longer wants to write ballet music or to play quartets in Russian society, and he wants to give up his post as

Inspector. In short he wants to live on income he does not have. I shall be bringing your okra seeds. But do not count on them. In France these creatures change their appearance and turn into frightful gherkins.

Yesterday I had two double encores, one for Grantzow and the other for a Little Russian dance.[5] The *aftor* (author) was recalled after each act but he only deigned to appear surrounded by the whole of his corps de ballet of *Mougiks* and others.

They had well deserved it. They all danced marvellously.

I am in the railway carriage with travellers for Tver and St. Psbg, or rather on board, for this line has two-storied carriages and beds, stoves, saloons, smoking room, a section for the ladies and a section for the gentlemen, and servants of both sexes serving you at table without your having to get out of the train. Such luxury makes you want to burst out laughing.[6]

A bientôt, from Fittingoff's house by the Bridge of Kisses.

Your very devoted

Saint-Léon

Moscow
1st December, R. St.

Louise[7], Minkus and Grantzow thank you and send thousands of good wishes.

50

To Charles Nuitter

Dear Nuitter,

I have been very slow in writing to you who are so prompt and keep your word to the end – this is a rare quality, just ask Delibes – since my return from Moscow, where I nearly froze to death, for the stove broke down at 10 o'clock in the evening and we had 17 degrees Réaumur of frost, with no fire and a high wind until 11 o'clock the next day. Never in my life have I been so cold. Relying on the stove I had left my heavy boots and the bearskin behind in Peters. Now I know better. Since my return I have had numerous discussions with Count Borkh, and in spite of everything I have been right. I was within my rights and thought I should stand up for them. I am working without respite, but in five or six days I ought to be able to see some light. But the Direction does not like seeing me breathing, and has sent Grantzow to me to be prepared for her début.[1] To stage *Giselle* and *Météora* is such a simple thing to them. Your friend danced Giselle on Thursday without any prior announcement, with an unbelievable success. The Emperor was present, and had her brought to his box and complimented her, saying that he was sorry she *preferred Paris to Russia*. They are all furious and angry with me. Never has there been such enthusiasm among the company. Tomorrow is her 2nd performance. The theatre is sold out. *Boudit poolnaï*[2], says the box office. Minkus, of whose laziness I only had a faint idea, arrives in a few days to finish and to supervise the last rehearsal. The time has come, I can do no more, my knees are cracking, my back is giving way, and I feel like a man of 70. This morning the Emperor turned up unexpectedly at the School, where I was rehearsing. He asked me questions and wanted to see how a scene and a pas were composed. My dancers did not know which way to look. Their shyness had no limits. He appeared amazed at the amount of work involved, and I took the opportunity of making a great show of my difficulties!!! Then H.M. got up and left to have dinner with the little girls of the School. What a terrifying experience for the cook, who was not expecting him. He asked for the best *kwass*, and ordered another.[3]

After visiting everywhere in the establishment the Emperor returned to the room where I was rehearsing and stayed for half an hour to see me compose and teach a variation to Mlle. Radina.[4] What an honour. When I had finished he took me into a corner and asked if I often came to the School. Every day, once or twice. He then questioned me on the behaviour of the young girls, whether they were regular in their attendance. I think he has had some bad reports. Then a quantity of Excellencies arrived, but when he saw them he immediately left the School.

If you had seen all those faces wanting to know what it had all been about, you would have died laughing. I said nothing to anyone. So I have composed a variation under the eyes of H.M. the Emperor. I quoted to him the words of the répétiteur Rochefort – still another to do but one less to come. He laughed. Bono. I have sent a telegram to M. Perrin. I cannot be in Paris before the end of January. Perhaps that will be too late. What can be done about it? However, if M. Perrin does not need me, I shall be much obliged if I can be told. I shall then stop off at Dresden, where they want me to put on three short ballets. That will serve as relaxation. Otherwise I shall cover the few leagues that separate us at the gallop. We are buried under snow. For a week we have had a glacial wind, a tempest. It whips along unceasingly, like needles sticking into your face. By a decree of the Emperor the Italian Opera has been abolished from next year. They say it has been done to get rid of the old relics here who draw up to 8,090 francs on good days. On Friday *Othello*[5] made 147 roubles, less than 500 fr., with Tamberlik, Barbot and Everardi. It is rumoured that Minister Adlerberg[6] is going to take an 11 month holiday. Count Borkh has resigned for the 3rd time. It is Suvarov, the furious Bogdanovite, who is going to take over the position of Minister of the Court.

The other evening I lodged an objection on behalf of Grantzow about the playbill, which had on it "First dancer of the I. Theatres of Moscow". I said that either they should put nothing at all or add "and the Paris

Opéra". The Gr. Duke Constantine[7] came up just when I was saying that on the stage and said, *"Paris takes no notice of us!!!!!!"* Those who are being watched, beware.

I close by wishing you all the happiness, success and profit you deserve.

Grantzow joins me, as well as Madame[8], in saying

Yours ever

Saint-Léon

18th December
1866
Psbg

51

To Charles Nuitter

Dear Nuitter,

I can only blame myself for not having written to you all this time. Difficulties rain down on me and mean increasing work to maintain the repertory.

First there was Grantzow's illness (a nervous fever) which kept her off the stage for a month. She made her return yesterday in *Météora*.[1] Not since the great days of Muravieva, who is Russian, have I been present at such a triumph. In spite of tripping on a badly closed trap she was able to continue in the most astounding manner.

From another quarter my ballet has been delayed by an accident that happened to Lebedeva in *Le Diable amoureux*. A spark from our untoward Jupiter fell on Lebedeva's eye. She has now been laid up for 18 days – and with her, naturally, my unbearable ballet.[2]

Mme. Petipa is the sole defender of the standard of Choreography. She has taken on a new lease of life since she has left her husband. Unfortunately her dancing has not improved. So here I am with 3 prima donnas on my hands!!! It is no small matter, specially now when the benefit season is approaching. Grantzow is to have another on the orders of H.M. They talk of giving her a present.

Delibes has written to me. I will answer him in a few days. Meanwhile please hand him the enclosed authority from Minkus who thanks him and will write to him as soon as he has *arranged* his last scene.

I have high hopes for the revival of *La Source* with Grantzow (although the ballet is on its last legs in France), for what has been missing is the woman, the ballerina.

A propos of Delibes' letter, tell him I think it is all a bit strong. I am always being told the same story of *honour* – there are no presents, no money for galas, and still less any Order of St. Andrew with 1,000 R. pension!!![3] I think we shall have to be satisfied with honour. They do not want to make any gifts to the Italian singers, and we share the same fate as the disgraced subjects of V. Emmanuel to avoid any jealousy.

The whole chorus and 68 orchestra players of the Italian Opera have been dismissed. The collapse is complete.

Since Delibes asks me how to send Minkus the money for the sale of the music, I will tell him. He merely has to go to M. Bazin, the notary, at 8 rue Menars and deposit the 500 francs in my name for Minkus's account, then let me know by letter, and I will act as banker!!!!! I will make the adjustment here. On Sunday there will only be five more weeks to go. I am thinking of having a rest in Paris and living on my savings. At least I shall have the pleasure of seeing a few of my friends again, among whom you will be one of the first.

I hope it will get milder by the time of my departure. My thermometer reads 24 degrees Réaumur this evening, and it is windy. Happily I have 18 degrees of warmth in my apartment.

The Emperor has been bear-hunting since yesterday. I hope he will not take it into his mind to have a ballet performed in one of his castles.

The ladies thank you for your good wishes, Minkus too. He is going to write to you on the subject of the libretto. Regards from all to all, and to you my friendly greetings.

A. M. Saint-Léon

18/1/67 R.St.
Psbg.

52

To Charles Nuitter

Dear Nuitter,

Yesterday 26/2 R.St. at 4.12 p.m. the curtain fell at the end of the 9th scene of the 64th performance of *Koniok Gorbunok*! In the evening at 11.22, the season ended with the 4th Act of *L'Africaine*. Today I have been to sign my engagement for two years with the variation of the term from 15th August R.St. to 1st January instead of for the entire season. The day after tomorrow I leave the Queen of the North with 29,000 fr. in my pocket. Grantzow leaves tomorrow. The railway carriage which will be her home until she gets to Prussia will be decorated with flowers, and at the frontier she will find a monster bouquet from the Petersburg public. Just imagine that in the six weeks after recovering from her ailments she has had a success that has surpassed everything since Elssler. At her benefit there was a storm of flowers, a gift of 4,000 fr. from the public, and a "very good" from H.M. Never have I seen or heard such enthusiasm. She is reengaged for three months in the season for two years at 36,000 fr, and *Météora, Fiammetta* and *Koniok* have been a series of triumphs for her. Full houses at every performance. Lebedeva has handed in her resignation and no longer wants to dance.

Finally my new ballet has not been given because of her. It is something saved for next season. Thank God I have finished! It seems like a dream, but in spite of everything this is still the only country for ballet. One just has to love it and return. Every day I look at the paper but I have not yet seen anything about *Don Carlos*. I shall probably arrive in time for the first performances.

Tamberlik has had an enthusiastic farewell in *L'Africaine*, Mme. Barbot thought she could risk taking a call herself after the 15th or 16th time that her Vasco was summoned, but the storm scene of the 3rd Act was immediately unleashed on the public. She made a sideward jump into the wings that was not without charm to escape from the public's view. The Opera is still to be abolished next year, and the ballet will support the Bolshoi Theatre on its own.

For the first time in three years we have had H.M. the Empress at the ballet, for *Météora*. H.M. sent a message to Grantzow by Prin. Wiasemsky that she had not enjoyed the ballet so much since Taglioni.

H.M. the Emperor applauded *standing* up in his box at the end of our "Source's"[1] benefit as she took her calls and, with the curtain raised, the ballet company presented her with a crown, while immense cheering echoed round the auditorium in the presence of H.M. Being charged with the task of presenting the crown, I held her by the hand. I felt she was going to faint, and for someone unaccustomed to such Northern excesses, that is really something. She *well and truly* wept and everything went off well. She will take a pretty packet away with her this year.

So, my dear friend, burdened with my okra seeds I shall see you, God willing and with the help of the railway engines, in *eight days' time*.

Until we meet, au revoir.

Yours ever,

Saint-Léon

28/2/67
Petersburg

17 degrees of frost Réaumur and mountains of snow –
but they love the ballet.

53

To Charles Nuitter

Dear Nuitter,

I have been told by Director Guedeonov[1] that Grantzow has signed, or at least is agreeable to signing, a
contract for 5 months a year for two years – for 69/70
and 70/71. That is why she has been unwilling to accept
M. Perrin's offer for eight months. The Director told
me he got for her 3000 roubles a month!! performance
bonuses of 50 roubles!!!! and a benefit with a 2000 R
guarantee for her!!!!!![2] It is quite Californian. Has anything been settled at the Opéra for this child of good
fortune? Mustapha Guedeonov, who pays so much to
his favourite dancer, does not have a penny to stage a
2nd ballet this season. It is probable, therefore, although
I dare not think of it yet, that I shall be paid my 8,500 fr.
to cast an eye over my old works. This ballet [3] will not
be put on until next season. If I do nothing good in
Armide[4] and for the 3rd act of the ballet, it will not be the
Direction's fault. Alas I dare not think of it. It would be
too much to expect. What a promised land, even with
its burnt forests, as if the train journey to the frontier is
not dispiriting enough.

I had counted on a change of climate, thinking it
would bring me some relief. I was mistaken. I suffer like
the damned.

I have seen Mlle. Dor[5] in *Le Corsaire*. She dances very
correctly, but is old-fashioned, if I can put it that way.
In my opinion she lacks charm also, and as for her

pantomime – *ni carascho*.[6] However she has had some success.

Here I am in my dungeon, perched on the 5th floor and seeing nothing but party tricks.[7] I am bored both out of doors and in, and at the theatre it is no fun. Petipa is working like a black.[8] His ballet will not be ready until October. Mustapha Guedeonov is very surprised that he has already had 60 rehearsals for his 3 act ballet. He will see many more of them.

I saw Taglioni's famous ballet *Flick et Flock*[9] in Berlin. It is a sort of faery with every known trick – out of date rococo groups, no delicacy, not a witty idea – and, if only one could forget it, the cocking-the-snook dance. It is unbelievable in that sort of theatre. There is much precision in the general dances. Mlle. Girod, who does not have an acting role, dances indifferently.[10] I saw Ribet in a Russian pas? All in all, not a favourable impression.[11]

I am thinking of writing to Delibes in a few days. Meanwhile best wishes from me. Please give my regards to everyone, and pay my respects to M. Perrin.

To you and to papa tante cosi.

Your devoted

Saint-Léon

19th September, Old St. Psbg

Bridge of Kiss . . . oh no, you know this dear address

54

To Charles Nuitter

Dear Nuitter,

You have put the finishing touch to your kindness this season by continuing to give me details about the performances of *La Source*, in spite of being perpetually busy. I wanted to answer at once, but I have been very hard at work. The new Director[1] wanted to engage Mlle

Salvioni but the poor woman has not had much rest since she has been here. She made her début in my new ballet last Tuesday.[2] The public is not friendly when one's name is not Salvionoff. It was particularly unjust towards her at the 1ère, the second performance was much better and I have no doubt that enthusiasm will follow shortly. In my opinion too the ballet is also one of the best. After the 1ère I did not feel it necessary to cut a single measure. It is extraordinary, for the Petersburg public I think it is a little too refined. Minkus had a success, and the scenery is splendid. The last 2 acts are being given at the gala for the marriage.[3]

You are probably in the throes of rehearsals for *Le Corsaire*.[4] I hope it will attract profitable receipts. You have told me of the arrangement made with Gord. I could not have been more touched, and will be much obliged if you would convey my sincere gratitude to M. Perrin. I shall shortly be preparing some little scenes with dances for Salvioni, intended for the Hunting Theatre. The Emperor has arrived, which will stir us into activity. Also Salvioni is learning *Faust*, and soon after I shall begin Grantzow's ballet.[5] Unfortunately, my dear friend, the health of your choreographer is deteriorating in a disheartening fashion. I am very ill. Minkus left today. He is sorry about his schedule and begs me to send his best wishes to you as well as to Delibes.

Please give my respects to M. Perrin, and my regards to Grantzow, to whom I shall be writing in the next few days, and to all who remember me, not forgetting Delibes.

Thank you once again for your two good letters, and accept the unchanging friendship of

Your devoted

M. Saint-Léon

2nd Oct. R.St. 1867
Ptsb.

To Charles Nuitter[1]

My dear Nuitter,

I have been so ill today that I am putting off my departure to Sunday evening. I shall see you tomorrow and will tell you the time of departure.

Please tell David père to come and see me before midday tomorrow.

Yours ever,

Saint-Léon

Friday

To Stepan Alexandrovitch Guedeonov[1]

Dear General,

Although I cannot be blamed either here or in Moscow for the delays in the works I have been under contract to stage, I nevertheless hasten to comply with your wishes in undertaking to have the ballet *La Source* (provisional title)[2] ready by 25th December of this present year instead of 10th December (stipulated by contract), on condition, however, that I can have sixty rehearsals between 16th August and 25th December.

Unforeseen circumstances, accident, illness, and hindrances beyond my control are in no way to make me liable.

Meanwhile I have the honour to remain Your Excellency's devoted

A. M. Saint-Léon

Petersburg
7/1/1868

To Charles Nuitter

Dear Nuitter,

I have just spent 71 days out of my bed in unbeliev-able pain. I could rest neither lying down, sitting, nor standing up. The only position which gave me relief was hunched up in a specially made arm-chair, and even then I could not bear that anti-choreographic exercise for long. The cause of this disaster is that I have been given in Paris and here a treatment completely unsuited to my illness. I have a complicated disease of the kidneys and the intestines.

Happily at this point I realised there is a God. A scene painter came to see me and recognised the very symp-toms from which he had suffered. He brought his doctor to me, and after a fortnight's treatment I slept in my bed for the first time on 27th December. I feel a marked improvement, and he hopes to cure me. It is in this sad condition, and with the help of choloroform, that I have done 3 acts of my ballet![1] Only one act remains to be done!!! Grantzow is also ill. You will appreciate, my dear friend, that I have not been able to busy myself very much with Delibes. I am going to make a start on it if there is no relapse; that would only bring on fatigue or too much over-excitement that could aggravate this frightful illness. When I am not working I am lying down all the time.

Let me know if the ballet will be put on before *Armide*, and if there is still a question of *Armide*[2]. When are they thinking of putting on *Faust*? Has M. Perrin, to whom please give my regards, ordered the set for the second scene?

I shall shortly be sending Delibes something to do. Has he finished the orchestration?[3] Hurry him up.

Happy New Year and good health, also to your father. Forgive me if I break off, but my head is spinning and I can no longer see.

Your very devoted

Saint-Léon

30/1/68
Psbg

58

To Charles Nuitter

My dear Nuitter,

I am very late giving you my news, but happily you know something of the routine of the Russian Theatres, and the beginning of the season is very heavy for the ballet-master, particularly if he is ill. *Koniok, Faust, Le Diable amoureux, Candoule, Zolotaia Ribka* and *Le Corsaire* have already been revived and staged. My ballet[1] is where it was when I left it, but much has been forgotten. Minkus is here and now I must press on with it.

I have thought out a way of shortening the 1st act of our work[2] by six minutes and giving it more life. Only Delibes will have some quite important adjusting to do. Although I am barely free of the bulk of what I still have to do, I shall copy out some guide-lines for Delibes which I will send you.

We will have the men drinking at table when the curtain rises. At the same time a number of dancers, men and women, enter from the back on the way, they say, to the Burgomaster. They lead the drinkers away to the music of the "Departure of the Sharpshooters", 2/4 etc. Everyone leaves. Antonia[3] comes out, is surprised at not seeing Frantz, goes to the window of her rival, of whom she is jealous, and begins to dance to attract her attention. (Existing waltz for the entrance). She hears a noise. It is Frantz. Antonia hides. Scene of Frantz with

110

the doll and Antonia as it is now, Then entrance of the crowd with the Burgomaster, with a man behind him bearing a banner decorated with flowers and ribbons and depicting a bell. He announces that the fête is going to take place, and invites the young girls to take part in it. They drink the health of the Lord of the Manor who has presented the bell, etc. All this is done to the Mazurka without many changes, even for the cast. He has Antonia brought on and asks her to dance as before. Pas de la gerbe, etc. Night falls. The people disperse, saying goodbye until they meet again next day at the fête. Exit. Then Coppélius etc. until the end. In my opinion the act will gain greatly by this – the sharpshooters and the second entrance of the crowd, which slow down the action for no purpose, disappear and nothing effective has been omitted. I do not know if you understand exactly what I mean, but I will write the scenes without the music, indicating the links. We shall have to prepare Delibes for this amputation, or rather this adjustment. The ballet will gain by it. I seem to have found an ending to the second act at last, without lengthening it by a single minute, since it will enable us to omit the dénouement in the March. At long last, in this way I shall have no more qualms.

One of these days you will receive a card of mine brought by one Bekefy, a dancer of Hungarian and Slav pas – in short, of pas de genres. His pantomime is not bad, and he is quite amusing in comic things. There are not enough men in the ballet company, and perhaps he would be useful. If he turns up, please speak of him to M. Perrin. I do not think he will not ask for much money, but he has a quality that our Zephirs in blouses lack in pas slaves. If he does not turn up, non ne parliamo piu. I nearly forgot, as a *danseur noble* he is not strong.[4]

Pugni has nearly died. He was in a wood, 16 versts from the city, owing 300 roubles to tradesmen. The Minister has paid this sum, and a collection among the dancers that produced 200 roubles is helping to feed him and his 8 children, 5 of whom are very young. He owes 8,500 roubles in all, and for twenty years he has been receiving 1,200 fr. a month plus a benefit etc.!![5] Dor has made her return.[6] 1st evening good, 2nd and 3rd poor receipts. Grantzow has announced that she has recovered, but as the Director is asking her to come before the 23rd September R. as is laid down in the contract, she has gracefully replied that she will do her best to arrive on the 25th. Funny girl!

Please pay my respects to M. Perrin and tell him that his speech was seized by the Russian customs, but happily the Minister, who was on the same train, walked past as I was arguing with these men. It was given back to me on the spot.

Many good wishes to your father, and to the ladies and gentlemen of the ballet. If Delibes is in Paris, my best wishes to him.

Your very devoted

Saint-Léon

14th September 69
Psbg.

Still the Bridge of Kisses!!!

59

To Charles Nuitter

My dear Nuitter,

Yesterday, 2nd November, was the première of my ballet *Le Lys* for the return of Grantzow[1]. 400 bouquets greeted our ballerina on her entrance in the 2nd act – the flowers being swept away and gathered up by the corps de ballet!!! and that by order. Finally 5 immense baskets of camellias and a dozen monster bouquets during what was a real Russian evening. She still has great charm and intelligence but between ourselves she no longer has those fine qualities she had at the time of *Giselle* and the

112

rehearsals of *La Source*. Finally, what was important to me was that yesterday's success was among the greatest I have had in Russia. After the 1st act, in which Grantzow does not dance, I was given a call, a rare occurrence at a première here. And later the same ceremony after each act.

Minkus's music is very good. Scenery and costumes very brilliant. No other ballet has ever caused me such trouble. I am worn out and very happy to have finished. I shall now get down to the specification of the changes to the 1st act.[2] Will not the opera of *La Coupe*[3] be longer than *Les Noces*?

Keep me fully informed about the preparations which M. Perrin is making with regard to the ballet. A free period is conveniently coming up at the very moment when M. Perrin will need me for the ensemble rehearsals and corrections. I am free to leave from 1st February and am consequently at his disposal, but the most important work must be prepared and I must be given a fortnight's notice. Delibes is probably not working? Hurry him up. Best wishes to all, do not rehearse too much, and if M. Justament[4] is willing to take charge of this boring task I can only be grateful to him. My kidneys and my sides are again very painful. I suppose it is caused by all the fatigue.

Madame asks me to send you and your father her best wishes. I also send mine, and shake your hand affectionately.

> Your very devoted
>
> Saint-Léon

3rd November 1869
Psbg.

Minkus, who left this evening for Moscow in spite of the delays that travellers are experiencing because of the burning of the Msta bridge[5], asks and begs me to remember him to you. He is on the point of finishing his *Don Quichotte* for Petipa.[6]

60

To Charles Nuitter

My dear Nuitter,

I am enclosing the cuts for *Coppélia*. The 1st version is the one I like least. The second, which I call the Caesarian, this one also by M. Perrin, is I think the boldest and has the best chance of being played.[1] I have spent much time coming to a decision, I have played everything many times over on the violin, and I think the 2nd version is good, as well as the ending, when one considers the ballet as a whole.

Kindly give the enclosed guide to our friend Delibes. The rough drafts are not numerous. Naturally only the length and the rhythm need be indicated, and indeed most are by him, taken out of his own score.

I tried out three endings. None of them satisfied me. After the Anglaise, a fanfare of trumpets on the stage, the immediate arrival of the Burgomaster with the friends of Antonia, who are half terrified that his fête will not take place. Everyone is grumbling. For a moment he is embarrassed, and then, realising that when all is said and done it is nothing more than a *lovers' prank*, or jealousy on the one hand and the delusion of an over-excited imagination on the other, he says to Coppélius, "Let us settle this matter later", and gives the lovers his blessing by embracing them and conducting them to the fête. The girl friends lead Coppélius away. March. Scene change. A short ceremony and divertissement. I have not been lazy, but this ending is the best. The other day I even tried out this scene with three mimes behind locked doors, and was pleased. All the other endings drag. Delibes wrote to me and I replied that I was still undecided. I have tried out several other versions, but looking them all over, I have come back to the second version. Entrance of Frantz and, at the dénouement, trumpet calls, as I have indicated. That makes a perfect contrast to the preceding scene. There are many beautiful things in his music. He need not worry. On the other hand one must think first of all of the general effect, and that the possibility of its being performed is helpful to the repertoire. A répétiteur of the two versions must now be prepared, ready for my arrival, and so let us say a few words about this arrival.

You have left me completely without news of Mr. Perrin's arrangements. Probably nothing has been decided yet. Is M. Perrin going to need me apart from the staging of *Coppélia*? When is he thinking of giving the ballet? In the event of M. Perrin not needing me apart from the ballet, I will try and do something to fill up the time and not waste too much of what I have earned here by living the life of a prisoner.

Never has Russia bored me more than now. I have decided not to prolong my engagement, which ends next season.[2] The weather is so dreadful this season that for the sake of my health I always have to stay at home as soon as I have finished rehearsing. M. Guedeonov wants me to remain here for the whole year except for 2 months' holiday, leaving me with all the work in Petersburg. M. Petipa would stay in Moscow. Good God, I will not stand for that. Then that devil of a rouble standing at 3 fr! All this makes me think. Add to that one of the most English spleens or *blue devils*, and you will forgive me for my Jeremiads. Just kindly ask M. Perrin in a few days time if something can be decided. If not, it is agreed of course that from 1st February 1870 I shall keep six weeks at his disposal as soon as he lets me know. M. de Dingalstedt[3] is planning that I should stage *Les Sept Corbeaux*, a German folk tale. I shall only enter into a contract with him if M. Perrin has no need of me beyond the staging of *Coppélia*.

The Emperor was present at the 5th performance of *Le Lys* and expressed his satisfaction, telling me to thank everyone concerned. He liked the pas du timbre, and I also arranged a coda that doubled the effect. Grantzow danced normally and seemed in good form.

Dor had her benefit yesterday with the revival of *Pharaon*[4], and what she danced in this interminable ballet (it began yesterday at 7.15 and we finished at 11.38)!! Oh Coppélia. It is unbelievable. She perspires and works like a dansophoble (sic). She does things that are so difficult that I wish they were impossible, for I have to look the other way, while as for charm, grace and wit, there is nothing there. I spent 15 days preparing this colossus and just for two occasions. Tomorrow is *Le Lys*, and Thursday *Pharaon*, the second time, for the benefit of a mime[5] and the last performance of Dor, who is going to Moscow.

Now *Pâquerette*[6] has to be staged for Grantzow's benefit. It will take me at least a month and some of my evenings. At last my health is a little better for the time being. In two months, God willing, I shall be out of this filthy place.

Give my regards to M. Perrin, and my compliments to all who speak of me. (Also, my good wishes from us both to Papa).

As for Delibes, tell him not to curse me too much, and to remember – cent fois sur le métier etc. etc.[7] It is for the common cause and it will be accounted for. In two rehearsals I shall do the 1st version for the Company. For the second version only the 2 first numbers of the 1st have to be omitted.

Forgive this horrible scribble
and believe me, your very devoted
Saint-Léon

29th Nov. 1869
Psbg

The old Russian princesses are in a state of great alarm. Their God, the almighty Mario, has just been crushed by the death of Giulia Grisi.[8] He has left for Berlin, and it is doubtful whether he will return.

61

To Charles Nuitter[1]

Paris Central, 9th January 70.

Delivered to addressee, No. 203.

PARIS PETERSBURG 3105 40 9 1 30 S = PARIS NUITTER DIRECTION OPERA = LETTER RECEIVED EVERYTHING AGREED EXCEPT THAT ARRIVAL DIFFICULT BEFORE END JANUARY WILL DO EVERYTHING POSSIBLE SUGGEST THAT PRELIMINARY WORK DONE QUICKLY IN PARIS WHICH WOULD CAUSE LITTLE DELAY TO SCHEDULE IF AT LAST RESORT ABOVE DATE ACCEPTABLE PLEASE TELEGRAPH WRITING TOMORROW = SAINT LEON

62

To Charles Nuitter

My dear Nuitter,

I am late in sending you the reply which I announced in my telegram. But how can I help it? The matinée performances are taking up all my time preparing replacements. I have got to the point of having to rehearse after the ballet for the Divs of the evening, either *Faust* or *Les Huguenots*, etc. Now at last we only have Saturday matinée, Sunday evening and Monday matinée, and it will be all over.

I received your last telegram, and everything is arranged. I shall leave on the 15th, R. St. If I can gain a day or two I shall use the extra time to travel more leisurely. As soon as I arrive I shall want to know what M. Perrin has decided about the cuts in the ballet, and almost at the same time I shall begin work on *L'Invitation à la valse*[1]. This delightful piece is a charming scene to choreograph, following the musical feeling very exactly. The music reveals or indicates the action. I am very pleased that M. Perrin has given me the opportunity of doing it.

You probably know that Grantzow has injured her foot rehearsing in the hall of the Conservatoire a fortnight ago today. It is not serious, but a little distension of the nerve always takes a month or five weeks to heal. It is a pity, for she was in good form and had been performing regularly. She no longer has the extreme freshness and elevation of the time of her début in *Giselle*, or during the rehearsals of *La Source*, but she is more of a woman than she was then and what with her delicacy, intelligence and grace, she is in short a very outstanding artist. She also has a certain elegance, and if she has a shortcoming, it is her modest technique, for which she *compensates* by little personal things from which it is possible to profit. As a change, she could be presented in a lively and playful guise which suits her very well. Apart from M. Perrin's project, I have two or three little ideas we can talk about; before she slipped I had begun to stage *Pâquerette*, in which she makes a mischievous peasant girl. I thought she was very good. Well, we can talk about all that.

I would be very grateful if M. Perrin would complete the roll of the corps de ballet as soon as possible. When I left there were quite a lot of gaps. True, it was summer and holidays are endemic at that time of year.

I was very pleased to hear of Mérante's appointment[2]. He is an intelligent and able artist and a delightful companion. Perhaps he will be able to help M. Perrin plug the holes that Coralli pointed out to me.[3]

This evening I was unable to attend the revival of *Les Huguenots*, which must have been very comical, like everything that is given at the Italian Opera here.

Mario, poor Mario[4], as Raoul, and in *Faust* and in everything. The opera would not bring in a pennyworth of receipts if it were not for the vogue for Patti.

118

The other day they gave a terrible pasticcio called *Esmeralda*[5], with Volpini, Trebelli, Graziani etc. at the première. Receipts were 1,200 roubles, a full house being 3,980. Rossini's Mass was coldly received.

I am in a hurry to leave, for the weather gets worse and worse all the time. There is much illness about.

Well, à bientôt, my dear friend, the interminable month of December – pendant to the month of August – finished only yesterday. A little patience and I shall hear the harmonious whistle of the railway engine. Meanwhile give my regards as well as my sincere thanks to M. Perrin.

Do not forget Delibes and your father
and believe me, your very devoted

Saint-Léon

1st/13th January 1870
Psbg.

63

To Charles Nuitter

I am answering your letter of 10th January to ask you to let Mérante make the provisional choice of the 3 ladies who are to replace Morando, Ricois and Nini[1], for on my arrival I want to have an overall look at everything to get a personal *impression*. Changes can be made afterwards if necessary. I do not know what M. Perrin has decided about the cuts in the 1st act, but for the ending of the 2nd I absolutely insist on my last version – trumpet calls, etc. This is the only way possible; otherwise it will always be long drawn out and cold.

Grantzow is not getting better, and I do not think she will be able to dance before February if all goes well. Unfortunately it is not a sprain but a *distension* of the muscle near the little toe in the left foot, which is worse. She is really unlucky. Hustle, hustle Delibes so that everything is ready on my arrival and we can attend to the changes, great and small, that have to be made.

With regard to the *Invitation à la valse* I cannot make it exactly as a pendant to my *Roses*[2] for it is less important, but in its Teutonic way it seems I shall have to *vergiss mein nichter* all that. Do not rehearse the 1st scene of *Coppélia* too much.

Yesterday I answered a letter from Minkus. He is quarrelling with everyone on account of the music for *Don Quichotte* which he was late in delivering. He has a beastly temper, but in May when he gets his pension he will cheer up. I opened the letter to send him your good wishes. Madame thanks you both for remembering her; she will arrive 4 or 5 days before me to attend to some business. The day after tomorrow I finish the rehearsals of *Teolinda*[3] which is to be given on Thursday, and then I am going to scheme so as to leave even before the 15th if that is possible.

A bientôt and all best wishes,
end of January French style

A. M. Saint-Léon

6/1/70
Psbg.

64

To Stepan Alexandrovitch Guedeonov

St. Petersburg
9th January 1870

Monsieur le Général,

Because of Mlle. Grantzow's unfortunate accident and the resulting dearth of the repertory, it is impossible for me to put together, this season, a programme for the half-benefit which is due to me each year under my contract.

I am therefore requesting Monsieur le Général the favour of granting me a full benefit, subject to deduction of expenses, next season, by way of compensation for the loss of my half-benefit during the current season.[1]

In anticipation of Your Excellency's decision I have the honour to remain, your very devoted

A. Michel Saint-Léon

Notes

Letter 2

1. Benjamin Lumley (1811–75) was manager of Her Majesty's Theatre, London, from 1842 to 1858. The early part of his management, when Jules Perrot was ballet-master, saw an exceptional flowering of the ballet.

This letter was written on 17th June 1844. The following day Perrot's *Le Délire d'un peintre* was given with the choreographer as the painter, and with "a new pas de deux" by Fanny Elssler and Henri Montessu. However, Lumley must have overcome Saint-Léon's objections because, as *The Times* reported, he did dance the pas de trois with Elisa Scheffer and Adeline Plunkett and produced "extraordinary bounds and never-ending pirouettes that were as wonderful as ever." Perhaps the fact that the Queen and Prince Albert were in the Royal Box with the King of Saxony was the swaying factor.

Letter 3

1. This letter, originally from the files of the theatre, bears the endorsement "1846 August. St. Leon relative Engagement." It refers, therefore, to the terms for the 1847 season.

2. Income Tax, which had been introduced in Great Britain in 1842 was then charged at 7d in the £ – about 3%.

Letter 4

1. Henri Duponchel (1796–1868), Director of the Opéra 1835-40 and, in partnership with Nestor Roqueplan, 1847–49. He had earlier been in charge of the mise en scène under Dr. Véron.

122

2. *Alma, ou la Fille de feu*, ballet in 4 scenes produced by A. J. J. Deshayes, with additional choreography by Jules Perrot and Fanny Cerrito, music by Michael Costa, created at Her Majesty's Theatre, London, 23rd June 1842. The role of Alma was one of Cerrito's finest creations.

3. The original London production was in fact only in four scenes: a palace of fire, a town in Germany, a ballroom in France, and Granada. For *La Fille de marbre*, as the ballet was renamed for the Paris Opéra production of 1847, the action was condensed into three scenes – the Palace of the Spirit of Fire, a square in Seville, and the Alhambra.

4. The pas de fascination, a brilliant pas d'action, was arranged by Perrot and originally danced by him and Cerrito. The choreography of the pas de trois was by Cerrito herself.

5. One of the Escudier brothers, Léon and Marie, who were at that time publishing the music magazine, *La France Musicale*, and running a theatrical agency.

Letter 5

1. Secretary-General of the Opéra.

Letter 6

1. Saint-Léon and Cerrito, supported by Adelaide O'Bryan and Adèle Chapuis, made three appearances at the Theatre Royal, Plymouth, on 25th, 27th and 28th August, and two at the Theatre Royal, Bath, on 31st August and 4th September. The four dancers stayed at the Castle Hotel when appearing in Bath.

2. Cesare Pugni (1802?–70) was one of the most prolific ballet composers of all time. Between 1843 and 1850 he was employed at Her Majesty's Theatre, London, writing the music for many of Perrot's most important ballets, including *Ondine, La Esmeralda, Eoline, Catarina* and the *Pas de Quatre*. Later, from 1851 to 1870, he was official composer of ballet music to the Imperial Theatres in Russia.

Letter 7

1. Saint-Léon and Cerrito were engaged for four or five months following the season at Her Majesty's Theatre, London, at a combined salary of 6,500 fr. a month, or a total of 30,000 fr. if the engagement was extended to five months.

2. France had been a republic since February 1848 when Louis-Philippe had been dethroned. Since then the political situation had been confused, and stability was not to return until December, when Louis Napoleon (afterwards Napoleon III) was elected President of the Republic by an overwhelming majority.

3. A reference to the multi-stellar divertissements which Jules Perrot had been producing in London. The most famous of these was the *Pas de Quatre* of 1845, but the reference here is to *Les Quatre Saisons*, created at Her Majesty's Theatre on 13th June 1848 with Fanny Cerrito, Carlotta Grisi, Carolina Rosati and Marie Taglioni the younger.

4. Joint Directors of the Paris Opéra since 31st July 1847. Duponchel retired in November 1849, and Roqueplan continued as sole director until 1854.

Letter 8

1. Pierre-Alfred Ravel (1811 or '13–1881), an actor who enjoyed great popularity at the Théâtre du Vaudeville and the Théâtre des Variétés. This letter was probably written in 1850.

Letter 11

1. Directeur de la scène at the Paris Opéra.

Letter 12

1. Saint-Léon's marriage with Cerrito had broken up in 1851, and on 21st July of that year he had signed a new engagement with the Opéra as maître de ballet and professeur for three years from 1st August 1851.

2. Roqueplan replied to this letter on 22nd December 1852, agreeing the terms for the cancellation of Saint-Léon's contract.

Letter 13

1. Gabriéle Yella (1835–57) was an Austrian ballerina who came from a good family and preferred to adopt the name of Yella, a diminutive of Gabriele, to using her real name of von Spielmann. She made her début at the Kärntnertortheater, Vienna, in 1851. In 1853 she appeared at the Théâtre Lyrique, Paris, in the opera-ballet, *Le Danseur du roi*, of which Saint-Léon was the choreographer: this letter of his dates from this period. She danced in St. Petersburg

124

from 1854 to 1855, and played the part of Giselle in Hamburg in 1855. The Russian dance historian Khudekov wrote of her: "Although her talent was far from first-class, she nevertheless found favour with the public. Yella never enjoyed European fame. This conclusion follows from ten of her letters in my collection. From these letters written to one of the Petersburg critics it is clear that she danced mainly in various minor German theatres. She describes successes which were not hard to achieve in Königsberg, Marienburg and Pest . . . Everywhere she was poorly paid, and therefore much appreciated Petersburg, where she was quite handsomely remunerated." She possessed an extraordinary gift for languages and became fluent in Russian in the short time she was in that country.

Letter 14

1. G. B. Benelli was a theatrical agent who carried on his business at 27 rue Olivier, Paris. The rue Olivier no longer exists, having been incorporated in the rue de Chateaudun.

2. Opera by Rossini. Marietta Alboni (1826–94) was one of the most celebrated contraltos of her time.

3. B. Belart.

4. Opera by Bellini.

5. Giuseppe Forti, tenor.

6. *Lucia di Lammermoor*, opera by Donizetti.

7. *Saltarello* was performed 47 times during Saint-Léon's two seasons in Lisbon.

8. The leading ballerinas were Louise Fleury, Julie Lisereux, Elisa Cantini, Augusta Dominichettis, Rosalie Lequine and Mlle. Marmet. The leading male dancer was Adrien Gredelue.

9. José Swift, tenor.

10. Opera by Bellini.

11. Francisco York was choreographer and dancer at the São Carlos Lisbon, from 1836 to 1843. He later went to Brazil. In 1854 he returned to Portugal, produced a ballet at the São Carlos and shortly afterwards was appointed director of that theatre. He soon met with financial failure, and was replaced in January 1855.

12. Vandris also danced in London, in 1856.

Letter 15

1. After York's departure, the Teatro São Carlos was managed by Vicente Corradini.

2. Opera by Donizetti.

3. Opera by Donizetti.

4. François-Louis Crosnier (1792–1867), director of the Paris Opéra from 11th November 1854 to 30th June 1856. His mother had been concierge of the Opéra for some thirty-five years.

5. Saint-Léon signed a new contract for the season of 1855–56. Under it he was to receive a salary of 1,644$000 reis (approximately 9,133 fr.) a month, out of which he had to pay the principal dancers he had brought from Paris. The ballet company was smaller than for the previous season, the principal dancers being Louise Fleury, Hortense Clavelle, Palmyra Andrew, Mariquita Moreno and Rosalie Lequine.

Letter 17

1. Tear in original letter.

Letter 18

1. Léon Escudier (1819–81) and his brother Marie (1821–80) were then in partnership as music publishers and concert and theatrical agents. Léon was the businessman, while Marie occupied himself with editing the magazine *La France Musicale*. They dissolved partnership in 1860, and in his later years Léon directed the Théâtre Italien, presenting there the first production in France of Verdi's *Aida*.

2. Now Timisoara in Western Romania.

3. Giovanna Pitteri, a Venetian ballerina, made a brief appearance at the Paris Opéra in 1859, danced at the Scala, Milan, in 1864, visited New York in 1872–73, and for a number of years (1869–70, 1873–76) was leading ballerina at the Alhambra, London. She died in poverty in Marseille.

4. Enrichetta Bosè was ballerina at the Royal Court Theatre, Dresden, in 1859. She danced in Florence in 1869 and 1872–73, in Vienna in 1871, and at the Scala, Milan, in 1868 and 1874.

Letter 19

1. This letter exists only in the form of a copy appended to a letter from the Paris theatrical agent, Charles Formelle, to Andrei Ivanovich Saburov, Director of the Imperial Theatres from 1858 to 1862.

126

Léo Delibes. (Bibl. de l'Opéra)

Saint-Léon towards the end of his life.
Photograph by B. Braquehais. (Bibl. de l'Opéra)

Vous êtes prié d'assister aux Convoi, Service et Enterrement de Monsieur **Charles-Victor-Arthur MICHEL**, dit SAINT-LÉON, décédé à Paris, le 2 Septembre 1870, à l'âge de 49 ans, qui se feront le Lundi 5 courant, à midi *très-précis*, au Temple, (rue Chauchat).

On se réunira au Temple, rue Chauchat.

De la part de Madame Françoise-Marianne-Raphaël CERRITO, dite FANNY. sa Veuve, et de toute sa Famille.

Invitation to the funeral of Saint-Léon, sent on behalf of Fanny Cerrito.

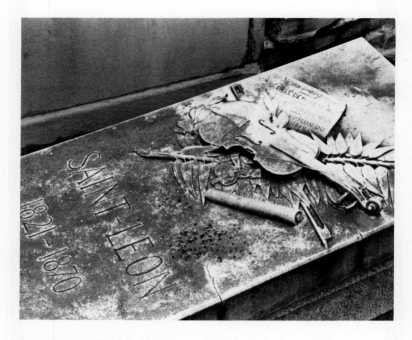

Saint-Léon's tomb in the Cemetery of Montmartre. Sculpture by
Belmondo (?). Photograph by Jean-Louis Tamvaco.

Letter 20

1. Emile Perrin (1814–85), Director of the Paris Opéra from 1862 to 1870. Before that he had directed the Opéra-Comique and the Théâtre Lyrique, and from 1871 until his death he was administrator of the Comédie-Française.

2. Marfa Muravieva (1838–79), one of the most promising of the younger Russian dancers. Born in Moscow, she was trained in St. Petersburg and became a soloist immediately on graduating from the Ballet School. After dancing in Moscow from 1860 to 1862, she returned to St. Petersburg where she created the leading role in Saint-Léon's *Théolinde* in December 1862, a triumph which was in Saint-Léon's mind when he wrote this letter.

The negotiations for Muravieva's engagement in Paris were complicated by intrigues in St. Petersburg, but Perrin was able to handle the situation by being kept well informed by Eugène Huguet, director of the Conservatoire de Danse of the Imperial Theatres. The principal instigator of these intrigues seems to have been Marie S. Petipa, who had danced at the Opéra in 1861 and 1862. In her efforts to prevent Muravieva's engagement she even persuaded Lebedeva's protector ("very influential with the management of the Imperial Theatres," said Huguet) to obtain leave of absence for Lebedeva so that she could take advantage of the situation and be engaged at the Opéra herself. These intrigues collapsed when Perrin made it clear that he was only interested in Muravieva.

Perrin decided that Muravieva would make her Paris début in *Giselle*, and would then appear in a ballet that was new to Paris. *Théolinde* was rejected because, having been seen in Paris as an opera-ballet (*Le Lutin de la vallée*) some years before, it would not have the appeal of a novelty. *Météora* was then proposed, but Muravieva's Paris creation in 1863 was to be *Diavolina*, which Saint-Léon produced with some haste.

To complete the story of the intrigue, Marie Petipa never returned to Paris. According to *L'Entr'acte* (15th April 1863) she was unable to fulfil an engagement at the Opéra-Comique owing to an injury sustained at Riga. Lebedeva did go to Paris that summer, but did not dance there. On her way through St. Petersburg she called on Huguet and frankly admitted that she wanted to dance in Paris, "*but*" – he reported to Perrin – "she is putting this off until next year if an opportunity arises at the end of next winter." Huguet recommended her as "a very distinguished artist; no one since Rosati has been a better mime than she." However, she was never to achieve her ambition to dance in Paris.

3. Comte Alexandre Walewski (1810–68), illegitimate son of

Napoleon I, was one of the leading French statesmen under Napoleon III. He was Minister of State from 1860 to 1863.

4. *Le Papillon*, choreography by Marie Taglioni, music by Offenbach, created at the Paris Opéra on 26th November 1860.

5. Originally produced in Lisbon, revived in St. Petersburg in 1861 and in Moscow in 1862.

Letter 21

1. Chief Accountant of the Imperial Theatres in St. Petersburg.

2. *Plamya Lyubyi*, created at the Bolshoi Theatre, Moscow, on 12th/24th November 1863.

3. Konstantin Lvov, assistant regisseur of the ballet company.

4. Saint-Léon's contract with the Imperial Theatres for 1863/64 entitled him to 7,500 roubles for the nine months from 16th August 1863 to 15th May 1864.

Letter 22

1. Marie S. Petipa (1836–82) was the first wife of Marius Petipa, whom she married in 1854. Her husband choreographed several of his early ballets for her. She lacked the technical virtuosity of Muravieva, against whom she intrigued with unrelenting vigour. She retired from the stage after separating from her husband.

2. Nadezhda Bogdanova (1836–96) was the daughter of the dancer and teacher at the Moscow Ballet School, Konstantin Bogdanov. He sent her to Paris on the recommendation of Fanny Elssler, and there she studied under Mazilier and in 1851 made her début at the Opéra under Saint-Léon's auspices in *La Vivandière*. She danced at the Opéra until 1855. She made her début in St. Petersburg in *Giselle* in 1856, and danced there and in Moscow until 1864. She retired in 1867 after guest appearances in Paris, Vienna and Warsaw.

3. The Emperor Alexander II.

4. Count Alexandre Mikhailovitch Borkh (1805–67), Director of the Imperial Theatres from 1862 to 1867.

5. *Fiammetta*, which was produced at the Bolshoi Theatre, St. Petersburg, for Muravieva's benefit on 13th/25th February 1864, was a revised version of *Plamya Lyubvi (Flamme d'Amour)* which Saint-Léon had staged for Sobeshchanskaya in Moscow in 1863.

6. In the event neither *Le Dieu et là Bayadère*, an opera-ballet by Auber created in 1830, nor *L'Africaine* was produced in 1864. The latter work, Meyerbeer's last and long-awaited opera, was not produced until April 1865, a year after his death.

Letter 23

1. Director of the Imperial Theatres.

2. Saint-Léon was engaged as guest choreographer at the Paris Opéra, where he was to produce *Néméa* for Muravieva. Borkh obligingly recommended that his request be granted, which it was.

Letter 24

1. Saint-Léon was awarded the first decoration on 20th April 1855, and the second in 1857.

Letter 25

1. Saint-Léon was awarded "the gold medal, to be worn at the neck, on the ribbon, of the Order of St. Stanislas" on 16th/28th May 1864. Ivan Frantsevitch Marcel was the régisseur of the ballet company.

Letter 27

1. Opera by Félicien David, created in Paris in 1859, and produced in Italian at the Bolshoi Theatre, St. Petersburg, on 27th January/8th February 1865.

2. *Koniok Gorbunok (Le Petit Cheval bossu)* had been created on 3rd/15th December 1864, with Muravieva as the Tsar-Maiden.

3. The Bolshoi Theatre, St. Petersburg, was then the home of Italian opera as well as of the ballet.

Letter 28

1. Saint-Léon was required by his contract to remain in Russia until the end of the season, but his presence was required at the Paris Opéra to arrange the divertissement in the forthcoming production of Mozart's *Don Juan*.

2. Two passports were held by each of them – a French national passport, and the passport issued by the General Governor of St. Petersburg. It was the custom of the Imperial Theatres to retain the passports of visiting artists during the term of their contract.

Letter 29

1. Adèle Grantzow (1845–77) was the daughter of Gustav Grantzow, a minor German ballet-master. She attracted Saint-Léon's attention when she was dancing in Hanover, and in 1864 went to study in Paris under Mme. Dominique. She was engaged as ballerina in Moscow on Saint-Léon's recommendation and made her début there on 15th/27th November 1865 in *Fiammetta*. She danced in Russia until 1873, her creations being Saint-Léon's *Le Lys* (1869) and Petipa's *Trilby* (1871) and *Camargo* (1872).

2. Praskovia Lebedeva (1839–1917) was the leading Moscow ballerina of her generation. She excelled in dramatic interpretation, a quality that was greatly valued in Moscow, but did not aspire to the technical virtuosity which was the forte of Muravieva, her contemporary and counterpart in St. Petersburg. Blasis wrote of her: "Through gesture and facial mime she expresses everything just as if it were said in words. Her dances are picturesque, brilliant, passionate and ravishing, if the role calls for those qualities." She was summoned to St. Petersburg for the 1865–66 season to replace Muravieva who had retired, thus creating the vacancy which Grantzow was engaged to fill.

3. *Robert le Diable*, opera by Meyerbeer, contained the famous Ballet of the Nuns which initiated the formula, so much used in Romantic times, of the ballet blanc. The leading part of Héléna had been created by Marie Taglioni in Paris in 1831.

4. Fenella, the heroine of Auber's opera *La Muette de Portici*, was a mime role which was generally played by a dancer. Lise Noblet had created it at the Paris Opéra in 1830.

5. Lebedeva had appeared in *Fiammetta* on the opening night of the Petersburg season, 28th September/10th October 1865. Her injury delayed the production of *Pâquerette*, which was not produced until 9th/21st December.

6. *Koniok Gorbunok*, in which Matilda Madaeva was playing the part of the Tsar-Maiden.

7. *Le Poisson doré*, based on a story by Pushkin.

Letter 30

1. Saint-Léon did not manage to produce this "short ballet."

2. The firm of Crait, which was founded in Lyon in 1823 and has been established in Paris since 1850 at 42 rue du Faubourg Montmartre, has been the accredited supplier of ballet shoes to the Paris Opéra since 1879.

3. The father of Louise Fleury.

4. Dominique Venettozza, Mme. Dominique's violinist husband; Louise Marquet, Maria Baratte, Léontine Beaugrand and Antonia Ribet, all members of the Paris Opéra ballet. Ribet was suffering from chlorosis.

5. Matilda Madaeva.

6. *Néméa* was in the Paris Opéra repertory from 1864 to 1871, and was performed a total of 53 times. In 1865 it was given only four performances.

Letter 31

1 The performances at the Bolshoi Theatre were then shared between Italian opera and the ballet.

2. The first production in Russia of Meyerbeer's *L'Africaine* was given by the Italian opera company in St. Petersburg on 7th/19th January 1866.

3. Caroline Barbot, French soprano-contralto. She had created the role of Leonora in Verdi's *La Forza del Destino* in St. Petersburg in 1862.

4. The revival of *Théolinde* took place on 9th/21st January 1866.

5. Grantzow had danced in *Météora* on 3rd/15th December 1865, and was to appear in *Giselle* on 28th January/9th February 1866.

6. Alexandre Arcadevitch Suvarov (1804–82), grandson of the great marshal.

7. Count Vladimir Fedorovitch Adlerberg (1790–1884), Minister of the Court from 1852 to 1872.

8. Nadezhda Bogdanova had made a single appearance at the Paris Opéra in *Giselle* on 13th November 1865. It passed almost unnoticed, and although she enlisted the support of Auber, Perrin did not engage her to dance again.

Letter 32

1. This letter was written in reply to a letter from Perrin (9th January 1866) saying that he has much confidence in Saint-Léon's judgment, asking when Grantzow can come to Paris and in what ballet she would make her début at the Opéra, and adding that he may ask Saint-Léon to do something for her after her début.

2. Lebedeva was to dance in *Théolinde* on 9th/21st January 1866.

3. Brother of the Tsar.

4. The first production of *L'Africaine* outside Paris was in London, at Covent Garden, where it was presented in Italian on 22nd July 1865. Michael Costa (1808–84) conducted, and was responsible for "an almost unprecedented amount of curtailment,

not greater, however, than what was necessary to bring its length within the bounds of English patience." (Harold Rosenthal, *Two Centuries of Opera at Covent Garden*, p. 146)

Letter 35

1. It is interesting to note that Saint-Léon appears to have collaborated with Minkus in the actual composition of the score.

2. Minister of the Emperor's Household under Napoleon III.

3. This occurred on 16th March 1866. Villaret had informed the management that he was unable to sing the role of Eléazor, and Mathieu took his place with only one rehearsal. He was continually hissed, and by the fourth act was so upset that he was unable to continue and the curtain was lowered.

4. Perrin put his name forward as a candidate for Director of the Opéra under the new arrangement, and was supported by many of the leading artists of the theatre. His application was successful, and he continued at the head of the Opéra until 1870.

5. The revival of *Don Juan* had its first performance on 2nd April 1866. The music for the divertissement, which was widely praised for its original and ingenious choreography, consisted, according to Gautier, of minuets taken from Mozart's symphonies and the *Alla Turca* movement from the Piano Sonata in A major (K. 331), orchestrated by Auber.

6. The principal singers in *Don Juan* – Jean-Baptiste Faure (Don Juan), Marie Battu (Zerline), Marie Sasse (Anna) and Eugénie Mauduit (Elvire).

7. *La Source*.

8. Created at the Théâtre Italien, Paris, on 19th March 1866.

Letter 36

1. Twenty-six years takes one back to 1840, but Saint-Léon did not put his name to any choreography until 1843.

2. Andreas Leongard Roller (1805–91), decorator and machinist in chief of the Imperial Theatres in St. Petersburg from 1833 to 1879.

3. *La Source*

4. It would seem that this request was not granted.

5. Théodore Guérinot (b. 1808) danced in Russia, first in St. Petersburg and then in Moscow, from 1834 to 1845. He produced a number of ballets in Moscow, mostly for Ekaterina Sankovskaya, whom he partnered. His wife danced in Russia under the name of Laure Peyssard between 1831 and 1849. He may have been the father of Regina Forli, whose real name was Héloïse Guérinot, and

132

who appeared at the Paris Opéra in 1839, as a child in *La Gipsy*, and under her stage name from 1852 to 1855. She was a pupil of Saint-Léon.

6. Emile Gredelue. His wife was a Mérante.

Letter 37

1. "Our child" is *La Source*, which Saint-Léon had more or less completed in Paris in the summer, but which he was unable to supervise in the last stages of preparation. The rehearsals had been prolonged because Grantzow suffered an injury in July (certified as "pain in the joints of the foot"). A request had been made through official channels for Grantzow's leave to be extended to the end of the year and for Saint-Léon to be permitted to remain in Paris until mid-September, but this was refused on account of the festivities that were being prepared for the wedding of the Tsarevitch (the future Alexander III). Guglielmina Salvioni was engaged to create the title-role in *La Source* in place of Grantzow, and began to rehearse it on 20th August. Saint-Léon had to leave for St. Petersburg the next day, and Lucien Petipa was entrusted with the final rehearsals.

2. Marius Petipa's new production of Mazilier's *Le Diable amoureux* was presented on 18th/30th October 1866 under the title of *Satanilla*, with Lebedeva as Satanilla. *Koniok Gorbunok* had its first Moscow performance on 1st/13th December 1866, with Grantzow.

3. The forthcoming marriage of the Tsarevitch and Princess Dagmar of Denmark, daughter of King Christian IX. She became known as the Grand Duchess, and later Empress, Maria Feodorovna, and was the mother of Nicholas II, the last reigning Tsar.

4. *Le Poisson doré*.

5. Saint-Léon uses the word "mouvement", possibly in the Italian sense.

6. Henri Mathieu (d. 1882) was one of the teachers of the Paris Opéra ballet. Edouard Pluque (1813–97), then a dancer of the Opéra, was to be régisseur de la danse from 1870 to 1895.

7. The danse du fusil was performed by Eugène Coralli, in the role of Mozdock, supported by the corps de ballet, in the final number of the divertissement in Act II.

8. Josef Mayseder (1789–1863), celebrated violinist and composer.

9. The Austro-Prussian War had disrupted the peace of Europe that summer, but peace had been signed when this letter was written.

Letter 38

1. The gala performance, which took place on 18th/30th September 1866, was in honour of the arrival in St. Petersburg of Princess Dagmar. The programme consisted of Act I of *L'Africaine* and Act II of *Fiammetta*.

2. In the last scene of *La Source*, Naïla, the spirit of the spring, sacrifices herself by giving her magic flower to her mortal rival. The flower awakens love in the latter's heart, but without it Naïla grows weaker and dies by the spring, which ceases to flow. Of Salvioni's rendering of the death scene, Paul de Saint-Victor wrote: "The agonising in the last act . . . assumes with her the importance and the splendour of a scene of high tragedy." (*La Presse*, 19th October 1866)

3. *Le Poisson doré.*

4. Alexei Bogdanov, who was at that time intriguing to obtain a position in Moscow.

5. It is not hard to detect a mutual antipathy between Saint-Léon and Lebedeva.

6. *La Source.*

Letter 40

1. The Pas du Hamac was the number entitled "Berceuse" (Act I, No. 5) in the final score.

2. This dance was to be entitled "Final. Danse Circassienne" (Act II, No. 18D).

3. More properly *"slushayus,"* an old-fashioned expression with a tinge of servility, meaning literally "I obey."

4. Nuitter had written the scenario for *La Fiancé valaque* which had been produced in Paris in November 1865. It was to be given at the benefit performance for Alexei Bogdanov, with Marie S. Petipa, on 11th/23rd November 1866.

5. The scenery store of the Opéra was then situated on the rue Richer, at its junction with the rue du Faubourg Poissonnière.

6. Blanche Montaubry, dancer of the Opéra.

7. All these dancers were featured in *La Source*. Eugénie Fiocre played Nouredda, Louise Marquet the gipsy Morgab, Maria Baratte Dadjé, Marie Sanlaville Zael. Léontine Beaugrand had an outstanding success in the divertissement in Act II.

Letter 41

1. The Empress Maria Alexandrovna (1824–80) was born Princess Marie of Hesse-Darmstadt. Her marriage with Alexander II

134

had originally been a love match, but they had drifted apart and the Tsar was at this time falling in love with the young Catherine Dolguruka, whom he was to marry after the Empress's death. The Empress, who never managed to inspire popularity in Russia, had a great love for the arts, and it was said only relaxed in the company of musicians and poets. The Maryinsky Theatre was named after her.

2. Massimiliano Graziani, composer of ballet music, had collaborated in writing the score of *La Fiancée valaque*.

3. This is not surprising, with four productions in preparation – *La Source* in Paris, *Le Poisson doré* and *La Fiancée valaque* in St. Petersburg, and *Koniok Gorbunok* in Moscow.

Letter 42

1. The Universal Exhibition of 1867.

2. Angelina Fioretti (1846–79), one of the leading dancers of the Paris Opéra, where she danced from 1863 to 1870. She had been trained at the Scala, Milan, and was a pupil of Carlo Blasis. She created the role of Thérèse in Lucien Petipa's *Le Roi d'Yvetot* (1865), and that same year Saint-Léon arranged a variation for her in Mozart's *Don Juan*. She left the Opéra after her marriage to the baritone Napoleone Verger. She danced at the Scala, Milan, from 1873 to 1875.

3. In April 1866 an unsuccessful attempt on the Tsar's life had been made by Dmitry Karakozov. After he was hanged, a number of men were tried on charges of being implicated in the attempt. One of these, Nicolai Ishutin, leader of a socialistic group at Moscow University, was condemned to death, and fifteen others were sentenced to exile in Siberia. After being reprieved by the Tsar at the eleventh hour, as Saint-Léon describes, Ishutin spent the remaining six years of his life in prison and forced labour.

4. The scenario of *La Fiancée valaque*.

5. *Le Poisson doré*.

Letter 43

1. Héloise Lamy (d. 1916), one of the dancers of the Paris Opéra, had been slightly burnt when her costume had caught fire in her dressingroom.

2. Simbirsk, now Ulianovsk, is a town on the Volga, celebrated today as the birthplace of Lenin. Saint-Léon may have been under the impression it was in Siberia!

3. The future monarchs of Denmark, Germany and England – Frederick VIII, Frederick I and Edward VII.

Letter 44

1. *La Source* had been given its first performance at the Paris Opéra on 12th November 1866.

2. *Diavolina* was the ballet which Saint Léon had produced for Muravieva during her first Paris season in 1863. According to *Le Ménestrel* of 12th July 1863 Pugni had borrowed airs from a collection of popular songs and elsewhere, and a polka-galop by Graziani, "*La Chasse aux hirondelles*", had been used for the *Ballabile des Canotiers*.

3. Princess Dagmar had been received into the Orthodox Church on 12th/24th October 1866.

4. The replacement of Grantzow by Salvioni.

5. Guglielmina Salvioni, Eugénie Fiocre, Léontine Beaugrand, Maria Baratte, Marie Sanlaville, Louis Mérante, Eugène Coralli, François Dauty and Edouard Cornet had all appeared in the first performance of *La Source*. "My beautiful gypsy girl" was Louise Marquet. Sacré was the chief machinist, Hainl the conductor, Despléchin one of the scene designers, Mathieu a teacher, Pluque one of the dancers, and Lormier and Albert the costume designers. Lucien Petipa had taken charge of the rehearsals when Saint-Léon had returned to Russia, and Francisque Garnier Berthier was the régisseur de la danse.

Letter 45

1. The first part of *Le Poisson doré* had been given at a gala performance at the Bolshoi Theatre, St Petersburg, that very evening, 8th/20th November 1866, with Lebedeva as Galia, Kantsyreva as the Goldfish and the page, Stukolkin as Taras, and Ivanov as Petro. The Crown Prince of Denmark and the Prince of Wales were present.

Letter 46

1. *La Fiancée valaque* had been given a second time at a gala at the Hermitage Theatre on 11th/23rd November 1866.

2. A younger brother of the Tsar.

3. *Severnaya Pchela (L'Abeille du Nord)*, a St. Petersburg daily newspaper. *Le Journal de St. Pétersbourg* was the French-language paper.

4. More properly *gotovo*, meaning "ready."

5. *La Tresse d'or* was a pas scénique in *La Fiancée valaque*, performed by Marie S. Petipa and Christian Johansson.

136

6. Ernestine Urban had created the leading part of Sofia at the Théâtre Italien, Paris, in November 1865.

7. No one is a prophet in his own country (*Nul n'est prophète en son pays*).

Letter 47

1. He was entitled to a half-benefit under his contract.

2. Alexei Bogdanov.

3. As a result of this protest, Saint-Léon received 2,000 roubles to compensate him for the loss of the half-benefit to which he was entitled in 1865/66.

Letter 48

1. Of *Koniok Gorbunok*.

2. A *pas de caractère* in Act II.

3. Probably Anna Sobeshchanskaya (1842–1918) who was to take over the part of the Tsar-maiden in *Koniok Gorbunok* on 9th/21st December 1866.

4. See Note 3 to Letter 40.

5. Nicolai Rubinstein (1835–81), younger brother of Anton, founded the Moscow Conservatoire. Jozef Wieniawski (1837–1912), Polish pianist, was the brother of the court violinist at St. Petersburg, Henryk Wieniawski. Anton Door (1833–1919), Viennese pianist, was then teaching at the Moscow Conservatoire. Honoré was a pianist and music teacher who was married to the singer of the Bolshoi Theatre, Moscow, Irina Ivanovna Honoré. Bernhard Cossmann (1822–1910), cellist, and Ferdinand Laub (1832–75), violinist, were both professors at the Moscow Conservatoire. Franz Czerny (1830–1900) was a well-known piano teacher. Ludwig Minkus (1826–1917) was, of course, the well-known ballet composer who was Inspector of Orchestras for the Moscow theatres.

6. Verdi's *Don Carlos* was in preparation at the Paris Opéra. It was given its first performance on 11th March 1867 with a divertissement arranged by Lucien Petipa.

Letter 49

1. Anna Sobeshchanskaya.

2. Count Borkh, Director of the Imperial Theatres.

3. i.e. to stage the divertissement in *Don Carlos* at the Paris

137

Opéra. Saint-Léon resolved his difference with the Direction, and it was Lucien Petipa who eventually produced it.

4. Might this be the seed from which *Coppélia* germinated?

5. The character dances in the seventh scene ended with Little Russian dance, which was performed in Moscow by Olga Nicolaeva and Alexei Kondratev with four supporting dancers.

6. Tver, a station on the St. Petersburg-Moscow railway. The city is now known as Kalinin.

7. Louise Fleury.

Letter 50

1. Adèle Grantzow made her St. Petersburg début at the Bolshoi Theatre in *Giselle* on 13th/25th December 1866.

2. More properly, *budet polnyi*, meaning "it will be full."

3. A Russian beverage, made from rye rusks, of a low alcoholic content and consequently suitable to be served to children.

4. Lubov Radina (1838–1917).

5. Rossini's opera *Otello*, with Enrico Tamberlick (1820-89), tenor, Caroline Barbot (b. 1830), soprano, and Camilla Everardi (1825–99), baritone.

6. Count Vladimir Fedorovitch Adlerberg was Minister of the Imperial Court from 1852 to 1872. He was to be succeeded not by Suvarov, but by his son Alexandre.

7. Brother of Alexander II.

8. Louise Fleury.

Letter 51

1. Grantzow appeared in *Météora* on 18th/30th January 1867.

2. In applying to be released from her contract, Lebedeva gave her reason as ill health, but a difference between her and the administration arising out of the production of *Le Poisson doré* was an important contributory factor. Her eye injury temporarily blinded her, and when she recovered her sight was considerably impaired.

3. The Order of St. Andrew, founded by Peter the Great, was the highest Russian order.

Letter 52

1. Adèle Grantzow, who was to play the title role of *La Source* on her return to Paris in the summer.

Letter 53

1. Stepan Alexandrovitch Guedeonov (1818–79) had become Director of the Imperial Theatres in 1867, after the death of Count Borkh, and was to hold the post until 1875. He was the son of Alexandre Guedeonov, Director of the Imperial Theatres from 1834 to 1858.

2. A note attached to this letter calculates Grantzow's salary and bonuses at the exchange rate of 4 francs to the rouble.

3. Presumably *Le Lys*.

4. Opera by Gluck. It was not produced.

5. Henriette Dor made her St. Petersburg début as Medora in *Le Corsaire* on 3rd/15th September 1867.

6. *Ne khorosho* – not good.

7. The meaning of this phrase – *ne voyant que de trucs* – is not entirely clear. Saint-Léon may have been referring to Dor's excessive reliance on feats of virtuosity.

8. Marius Petipa was working on *Le Roi Candaule,* which was first performed on 17th/29th October 1867 with Henriette Dor.

9. *Flick und Flock's Abentheuer*, comic ballet in 3 acts and six scenes, choreography by Paul Taglioni, music by Hertel, was created at the Royal Berlin Opera on 20th September 1858.

10. Maria (or Marietta) Girod danced in Berlin from 1866 to 1868. She danced also at the Scala, Milan, in 1866 and 1867, at Covent Garden, London, in 1872, and in Vienna in 1873.

11. Antonia Ribet (1848–71), a product of the Ecole de Danse of the Paris Opéra, had left the Opéra to accept an engagement in Berlin. She died in Alger.

Letter 54

1. S. A. Guedeonov.

2. The complete version of *Le Poisson doré* was first given at the Bolshoi Theatre, St. Petersburg, on 26th September/8th October 1867, with Salvioni making her Russian début as Galia.

3. The gala took place on 18th/30th October 1867. Salvioni appeared in scenes 4 and 6 of *Le Poisson doré*.

4. *Le Corsaire*, which had originally been produced by Mazilier for Rosati at the Paris Opéra in 1856, was revived there for Grantzow on 21st October 1867.

5. Salvioni appeared in Perrot's ballet *Faust* at A. N. Bogdanov's benefit on 2nd/14th January 1868. Grantzow made her reappearance on 5th/17th December 1867 in *Météora*.

Letter 55

1. This letter, written on notepaper headed with the address 21 rue Laval, Paris, is undated, but was probably written in about September 1868.

Letter 56

1. Director of the Imperial Theatres from 1867 to 1875.
2. This project did not materialize. *La Source* was never revived in Russia.

Letter 57

1. *Le Lys.*
2. Gluck's *Armide* was not in fact produced at the Opéra. Gounod's *Faust* was to be the operatic event of 1869.
3. Delibes was then composing the music for *Coppélia.*

Letter 58

1. *Le Lys.*
2. *Coppélia.*
3. The name of the heroine was to be changed from Antonia to Swanilda, The first act was tightened still further, and eventually opened with Swanilda's entrance onto an empty stage.
4. Alfred Bekefy (1843–1925) had a long and distinguished career as a character dancer in both St. Petersburg and Moscow.
5. Further evidence of Pugni's financial problems is to be found in a letter to Marius Petipa which the latter reproduced in his memoirs. A pathetic postscript to this letter, written in 1860, makes this plea: "Tearfully I ask you to send some money; I am without a sou."
6. In Petipa's *Le Roi Candaule* on 31st August/11th September 1869.

Letter 59

1. *Le Lys* was first performed on 21st October/2nd November 1869. It was the first ballet which Grantzow created. It was based on a Chinese story, and Minkus re-used much of the music he had composed for *La Source.*
2. Of *Coppélia.*

140

3. Perhaps a reference to Eugène Diaz's opera *La Coupe du roi de Thule*, which was to be produced at the Paris Opéra in January 1873.

4. Henri Justament had succeeded Lucien Petipa as *premier maître de ballet* of the Opéra in 1868. He was only to produce one work there – the ballet in Gounod's opera *Faust* – and was to be succeeded by Louis Mérante in 1869.

5. The railway line from St. Petersburg to Moscow crosses the Msta River about a hundred miles from St. Petersburg.

6. *Don Quichotte*, grand ballet in 4 acts and 8 scenes, choreography by Marius Petipa, music by Minkus, created at the Bolshoi Theatre, Moscow, on 14th/26th December 1869. A revised version was produced in St. Petersburg in 1871.

Letter 60

1. The "Caesarian" version was probably that in which the opening of Act I was cut so that Swanilda made her entrance onto the empty stage.

2. Saint-Léon's two-year agreement, to which he referred in Letter 52, had obviously been extended to cover the 1870-71 season.

3. Franz von Dingelstedt was at this time Director of the Hofoper in Vienna.

4. Petipa's *La Fille du Pharaon*, originally produced in 1862.

5. Alexei Bogdanov. The benefit performance in fact took place on Sunday 7th/19th December 1869.

6. *Pâquerette* was not produced because Grantzow fell ill and was unable to dance from the beginning of January to the middle of February 1870.

7. A reference, slightly misquoted, to Boileau's *L'Art Poétique* (I, 172–173):

Vingt fois sur le métier remettez votre ouvrage;
Polissez-le sans cesse et le repolissez.

8. Giulia Grisi, the celebrated soprano and wife of the tenor Mario, died in Berlin on 29th November 1869.

Letter 61

1. Nuitter had telegraphed to Saint-Léon on 4th January 1870 asking if he could come to Paris before February. To this telegram of Saint-Léon, Nuitter replied on 10th January: "Return end January in order. Director agrees with thanks."

Letter 62

1. Saint-Léon was to produce the divertissement in the new production of Weber's opera *Le Freychütz*, using Berlioz's orchestration of "*L'Invitation à la danse.*"

2. Louis Mérante (1828–87) had been nominated to succeed Henri Justament as premier maître de ballet of the Opéra. He held the post until his death, and produced many successful ballets including *Sylvia* (1876), *La Korrigane* (1880) and *Les Deux Pigeons* (1886).

3. Eugène Coralli, son of the choreographer Jean Coralli, was *régisseur de la danse* from 1867 to 1870.

4. In *Les Huguenots*, opera by Meyerbeer.

5. *Esmeralda*, opera by Fabio Campana, specially written for Adelina Patti, created at the Bolshoi Theatre, St. Petersburg, on 18th/30th December 1869.

Letter 63

1. Carlotta Morando, Blanche Ricois (later Righetti) and Theresina Nini, dancers of the Opéra.

2. *Les Roses* was a divertissement which Saint-Léon had arranged for *Le Lys*.

3. *Théolinde* was performed on 8th/20th January 1870 with Vazem.

Letter 64

1. Saint-Léon's request was granted, but he was to die before the 1870/71 season.

APPENDIX I

The Ballets of Saint-Léon

1843   *La Vivandiera ed il Postiglione*
        Music: Enrico Rolland
        Choreography in collaboration with Fanny Cerrito
        First perf.: Teatro Alibert, Rome, 26 Nov. 1843
        Revived at Her Majesty's Theatre, London, 23 May 1844,
           with music by Cesare Pugni (whose score was used in
           later revivals) and choreography attributed to Cerrito
           alone.
        Other revivals : 1844 – Bologna, 1846 – Berlin, 1848 –
           Venice, Paris, 1849 – Königsberg, 1853 – Vienna, 1855 –
           Lisbon, St. Petersburg (produced by Perrot), 1858 –
           Pest. Also revived in Bordeaux, Hamburg.

1845   *Rosida, ou les Mines de Syracuse*
        Music: Cesare Pugni
        First perf. : Her Majesty's Theatre, London, 29 May 1845
        Attributed on the playbill to Saint-Léon alone, but by
           Lumley in his memoirs to Cerrito. It was doubtless a
           work of collaboration.
        Included *La Sicilienne*, which was later to be incorporated
           into *Stella* (q.v.), and *La Wolinienne*, which Saint-Léon
           later used in *Le Danseur du roi* (q.v.)

1846   *Der Maskenball*
        Choreography in collaboration with Cerrito
        First perf. : Kön. Theater, Berlin, 22 Apr. 1846

1847   *Das Blümenmädchen im Elsass*
        Music : Massimiliano Graziani, Conradi
        First perf. : Kön. Theater, Berlin, 27 Feb. 1847
        La Fille de marbre
        Music : Cesare Pugni, after Michael Costa
        A rearrangement of *Alma*, produced in London, 1842
        First perf. : Opéra, Paris, 20 Oct. 1847

Revivals : 1855 – St. Petersburg (produced by Perrot). Also revived in Hamburg. *Sataniel ou a estatua encantada* (São Carlos, Lisbon, 29 Oct. 1855) may be another revival.

1848   *Tartini il Violinista*
Music : Saint-Léon, Giovanni Felis, Cesare Pugni (Act II)
First perf. : Gran Teatro La Fenice, Venice, 29 Feb. 1848
Revivals : 1849 – Paris (as *Le Violon du Diable*), Königsberg, 1851 – Madrid, 1854 – Vienna (as *Die Teufelsgeige*), 1855 – Lisbon, Oporto, 1859 – Augsberg, Magdeburg, Brunswick. Also revived in Bordeaux, Brussels, Dresden, Amsterdam, Hamburg.
The divertissement, *Les Fleurs animées*, from this ballet was sometimes given on its own.

L'Anti-Polkista ed i Polkamani
First perf. : Gran Teatro La Fenice, Venice, 28 Mar. 1848
Revival : 1855 – Oporto

1850   *Stella*
Music : Cesare Pugni
First perf. : Opéra, Paris, 22 Feb. 1850
Revivals : 1851 – Madrid, 1853 – Vienna

Menuet, Gavotte et Polka, ou Jadis et aujourd'hui
First perf. : Grande Salle du Conservatoire, Paris, 23 Apr. 1850.

L'Enfant prodigue (divertissement in Auber's opera)
First perf. : Opéra, Paris, 6 Dec. 1850
Revival : 1854 – Vienna

1851   *Pâquerette*
Music : François Benoist
Scenario : Théophile Gautier
First perf. : Opéra, Paris, 15 Jan. 1851
Revivals : 1854 – Vienna, 1855 – Lisbon, 1858 – Turin, 1860 – St. Petersburg (music by Benoist and Pugni). Also revived in Dresden

Les Nations (cantata by Adolphe Adam)
First perf. : Opéra, Paris, 6 Aug. 1851

1852   *Le Berger Aristée et les abeilles* (divertissement in Halévy's opera *Le Juif errent*)
First perf. : Opéra, Paris, 23 Apr. 1852
Revivals : 1854 – Lisbon, 1858 – Königsberg, Tilsit, Vienna (as *Die Macht der Tone*), Pest, 1859 – Magdeburg, St. Petersburg. Also revived in Dresden.

1853   *Le Lutin de la vallée* (opera ballet with music by Ernest Gautier)
First perf. : Théâtre Lyrique, Paris, 22 Jan. 1853

Revivals : 1855 – Lisbon (as a ballet for the first time), Oporto, 1858 – Königsberg (music attributed to Saint-Léon, Pugni, Bartay), Vienna, Stuttgart, 1859 – Munich. Also revived in Brussels, Hanover.

Later produced as a ballet under the title *Théolinde l'orpheline* (q.v.)

Le Danseur du roi (opera ballet with music by Ernest Gautier)

First perf. : Théâtre Lyrique, Paris, 22 Oct. 1853

Later produced as a ballet under the title *Saltarello* (q.v.)

1854   *La Roziere*

First perf. : Teatro de São Carlos, Lisbon, 13 Oct. 1854.

Saltarello, ou o maniaco po la dança

Music : Saint-Léon

A revised version, as a ballet, of *Le Danseur du roi* (1853), q.v.

First perf. : Teatro de São Carlos, Lisbon, 29 Oct. 1854

Revivals : 1855 – Oporto, 1858 – Tilsit, Vienna, Pest, Stuttgart, 1859 – Munich, St. Petersburg, 1860 – Moscow, 1865 – Paris (as *Don Zeffiro*, produced by Gredelue). Also revived in Dresden, Hanover.

Lia la bayadère

First perf. : Teatro de São Carlos, Lisbon, 14 Nov. 1854.

1855   *O ensaio geral, ou as afflicçoés de Zefferini*

Music : adapted by Saint-Léon from various composers

First perf. : Teatro de São Carlos, Lisbon, 2 Feb. 1855

Revivals : 1862 – St. Petersburg (as *Les Tribulations d'une répétition générale*, music by ★★★ [i.e. Saint-Léon] and Pinto). Also revived in Dresden.

Bailados allegoricos

First perf. : Teatro de São Carlos, Lisbon, 17 Sep. 1855.

1856   *O Triumvir amoroso, ou muitos espinhos e nenhuma rosa*

First perf. : Teatro de São Carlos, Lisbon, 25 Jan. 1856

Os Saltimbancos, ou os processo do fandango

Music : orchestrated by Santos Pinto

First perf. : Teatro de São Carlos, Lisbon, 20 Apr. 1856

Revivals : 1858 – Vienna (renamed *Jahrmarkt zu Haarlem*, music attributed to Pinto, Saint-Léon and Strebinger), Dresden (music attributed to Saint-Léon), 1861 – St. Petersburg (renamed *La Perle de Séville*, music by ★★★ [i.e. Saint-Léon], Pinto and Pugni).

Meteora, ou as estrellas cadentes

Music : Santos Pinto

First perf. : Teatro de São Carlos, Lisbon, 9 May 1856

Revivals : 1861 – St. Petersburg (music attributed to ★★★

[i.e. Saint-Léon], Pinto and Pugni), 1862 – Moscow (produced by Carlo Blasis, music attributed to Pinto and Pugni).

Stradella, ou o poder da musica
First perf. : Teatro de São Carlos, Lisbon, 19 May 1856

1859   *Jovita, ou les Boucaniers mexicains*
Music : Théodore Labarre
A reworking of the ballet produced by Joseph Mazilier at the Opéra, Paris, in 1853.
First perf. : Bolshoi Theatre, St. Petersburg, 13/25 Sept. 1859

1860   *Graziella, ou les Dépits amoureux*
Music : Cesare Pugni
First perf. : Bolshoi Theatre, St. Petersburg, 11/23 Dec. 1860.
(Previously performed at the Gachina Theatre)

1861   *Nymphes et Satyre*
Music : Cesare Pugni
First perf. : Bolshoi Theatre, St. Petersburg, 26 Oct./7 Nov. 1861

1862   *Théolinde l'orpheline, ou le Lutin de la vallée*
Music : Cesare Pugni
A revised version of *Le Lutin de la vallée* (1853), q.v.
First perf. : Bolshoi Theatre, St. Petersburg, 6/18 Dec. 1862
Saint-Léon used several dances from this ballet in other works : the *Hungaria* and the *Pas des Lucioles* in *Néméa* (q.v.) and *Plamya Lyubvi* (q.v.), the Wallachian wedding dance and the Friska in *Plamya Lyubvi*.
Revival : the Dance of the Elements was staged by Gredelue in Paris, 1866, as *Gli Elementi*.

1863   *Diavolina*
Music : Cesare Pugni
First perf. : Opéra, Paris, 6 July 1863
Based on *Graziella* (q.v.), incorporating the *Scène du filet* and *La Scarpetta* from that ballet, and *Le Bon vieux temps* from the St. Petersburg production of *Pâquerette*. The *Pas du Tambour* may be the same as the *Pas du Tambour de la Reine* from the Russian production of *Pâquerette*

Plamya Lyubvi, ili Salamandra
Music : Ludwig Minkus
First perf. : Bolshoi Theatre, Moscow, 12/24 Nov. 1863
Saint-Léon reworked this ballet for St. Petersburg as *Fiammetta* (q.v.) and for Paris as *Néméa* (q.v.). Dances common to all three were the *Berceuse, La Langage des*

146

fleurs and the *Chanson à boire*. The scene, *Naissance de Fiammetta*, appears as *Nascita della Fiamma d'Amore* in the Trieste revival.

Revival : 1868 – Trieste

1864   *Fiammetta, ou l'Amour du Diable*
Music : Ludwig Minkus
First perf. : Bolshoi Theatre, St. Petersburg. 13/25 Feb. 1864
A reworking of *Plamya Lyubvi* (q.v.). See also previous note on *Théolinde*.

Néméa, ou l'Amour vengé
Music : Ludwig Minkus
Scenario : Henri Meilhac, Ludovic Halévy
First perf. : Opéra, Paris, 11 July 1864
A reworking of *Fiammetta* (q.v.). The *Danse de la Noce Hongroise* was probably the same as the *Hungaria* in *Théolinde* (q.v.) and *Plamya Lyubvi* (q.v.). *La Coquetterie* was no doubt part of the scene, *Naissance de Fiammetta*, in *Fiammetta*.

Koniok Gorbunok, ou la Tsar-Diévitza
Music : Cesare Pugni
Based on the popular Russian tale by P. Ershov
First perf. : Bolshoi Theatre, St. Petersburg, 3/15 Dec. 1864
Revival : Bolshoi Theatre, Moscow, 1/13 Dec. 1866.

1865   *Il Basilico*
Music : Massimiliano Graziani
Scenario : Etienne Trefeu
First perf. : Théâtre Italien, Paris, 18 Nov. 1865, produced by Gredelue
Revivals : 1867 – Moscow (produced by Frédéric), 1869 – St. Petersburg (music by Graziani and Pugni)
Included the Spanish dance *La Nia-nia* from *Diavolina*.

1866   *La Fidanzata valacca*
Music : Massimiliano Graziani, Rodolfo Mattiozzi
Scenario : Charles Nuitter
First perf. : Théâtre Italien, Paris, 18 Nov. 1865, produced by Gredelue
Derived from the *Pas des Noces Wallaques* in *Théolinde*, included the *Friss valaque* from that ballet.
Revivals : 1866 – St. Petersburg, 1867 – Moscow (produced by Frédéric)

La Source
Music : Ludwig Minkus, Léo Delibes
Scenario : Charles Nuitter

First perf. : Opéra, Paris, 12 Nov. 1866
Le Poisson doré
Music : Ludwig Minkus
Based on a story by Pushkin
First perf. : Part I only, Bolshoi Theatre, St. Petersburg, 8/20 Nov. 1866, complete ballet, Bolshoi Theatre, St. Petersburg, 26 Sep./8 Oct. 1867

1869   *Le Lys*
Music : Ludwig Minkus
Based on the folk tale, *Three Arrows*
First perf. : Bolshoi Theatre, St. Petersburg, 21 Oct./2 Nov. 1869

1870   *Robert le Diable* (divertissement in Meyerbeer's opera)
First perf. : Opéra, Paris, 7 Mar. 1870
Le Freychütz (divertissement in Weber's opera)
Music used : *L'Invitation à la valse*, arr. by Berlioz
First perf. : Opéra, Paris, 25 May 1870
Coppélia, ou la Fille aux yeux d'email
Music : Léo Delibes
Scenario : Charles Nuitter
First perf. : Opéra, Paris, 25 May 1870

Saint-Léon's own list, preserved at the Archives Nationales, also includes the following productions of ballets attributed to other choreographers:

Ondine (Perrot/Cerrito) : Bordeaux, Breslau, Dresden, Königsberg, Hamburg, Pest, St. Petersburg
Vincito al lotto (Cerrito) : Rome, Florence (1845).
Elève de l'Amour (Cerrito, f.p. London 1841) : Florence, Venice, Berlin
Giselle (Perrot/Coralli) : Turin, Königsberg
Esmeralda (Perrot) : Königsberg
Pouvoir de l'art : Vienna
Danses du Folletto : Turin
Le Prophète (opera by Meyerbeer) : Turin
L'Africaine (opera by Meyerbeer) : Dresden

148

APPENDIX II

Musical Compositions of Saint-Léon

The first forty-nine pieces appear on a manuscript list prepared by Saint-Léon himself, now in the Archives Nationales, AJ¹³499. At the foot of the list appear the words, "Molto favoro ma poco denaro." The dates in parenthesis give the earliest year of performance, so far as can be ascertained from playbills.

Compositions for the violin

1. *Ne m'oubliez pas*, romance sans paroles (1841).
2. Fantaisie sur un thème hollandais et sur la romance de *Guido et Ginevra* (1841).
3. *L'Appassianato*, air varié précédé par une adage sentimentale (1841). Op. 4.
4. Scena cantante sur thèmes de *Lucie de Lammermoor* (1840). Op. 3.
5. Grande fantaisie sur thèmes de *Lucrezia Borgia* (1842). Op. 7.
6. *La Romanesca*, air de danse du 16e siècle. (1842).
7. Fantasia e Concerto di violino sopra motivi di *Guglielmo Tell* (1842). Op. 17.
8. *Le Martele*, sur un thème de Beethoven (1844). Op. 10.
9. *La Voix d'outre tombe*, élégie.
10. *Le Soir*, nocturne (1841). Op. 14
11. *Le Rêve*, méditation (printed). Op. 11.
12. *Rondo*, barcarolle (1841, rearranged 1863). Op. 18.
13. Final d'*Ernani* (trans.). Op. 19.
14. *Une Matinée en Savoie* (or *Une Matinée à la campagne*), imitations burlesques:
    1 – L'Orage, 2 – Le Chant des Oiseaux, 3 – L'Heure, 4 – La Grange qui s'ouvre, 5 – Les Batteurs de blé, 6 – La Scie, 7 – La

Pompe, 8 – La Cloche et march des paysans, 9 – La Messe, 10 – Danse des Savoyards (1844). Op. 20.

15. Concertino sur *Jérusalem*. Op. 21.
16. *Mazurka pathétique*.
17. *Nel cor piu non mi sento* (Paisiello), air varié (1858). Op. 23
18. *Concertino romantique*. (Possibly the same as *Concerto en mi mineur*, 1845, or *Concerto Romantique* No. 1, 1858). Dedicated to Don Fernando, King-Regent of Portugal.
19. *La Guêpe et la Pervenche*, pastorale burlesque. Dedicated to the Emperor of Brazil (1853). Op. 18.
20. *Dernières illusions*, élégie. Op. 30.
21. *Glückstrahlen*, élégie.
22. *Express Train*, caprice burlesque (1853–54). Op. 31
23. *Sérénade espagnole*, boléro (1854). Op. 32.
24. *Il Pizzicato*, air varié sans archet (1854, completed 1860–61). Op. 33.
25. *Dodo*, berceuse burlesque (1854). Op. 34.
26. *Ballade à Terpsichore* (composed for the ballet *Saltarello*) (1855).
27. *Rataplan*, fantaisie sur *La Fille du régiment* (1857). Op. 37.
28. *Impromptu élégiaque* sur "Die schönsten Augen" de Stigelli (1861). Op. 39.
29. *Saint-Cécile*, mélodie réligieuse avec adaptation de la sour-dine-orgue (1859).
30. *Fantaisie Russe* No. 1 sur une chanson tzigane (1861).
31. *Une Nuit à Naples* (1853).
32. *Fantaisie Russe* No. 2 sur Kamarinskaya et un air petit Russien (d'après Glinka) (1861–62). Op. 44.
33. *Hungaria*, morceau de salon (1861). Op. 42.
34. *Il Bacio*, caprice.
35. *1ᵉʳ Quatuor* (Urématique) in E minor (1861–62). Op. 45.
36. *2ᵉ Quatuor* (Rococo) (1862). Op. 46.
37. *Valse élégiaque* (1863).
38. *Elien*, marche à la Hongroise.
39. *Gretchen, ou le Violon de Crémone* (pour sourdine-orgue) (1859).

For viole d'amour

40. *Chanson du Basque*.
41. *Souvenir des Huguenots* (1862).
42. *Le Palefroi de la Châtelaine*.
43. *Mal du pays*.
44. *L'Extase*, entr'acte.
45. *Invitation à la Valse* (Weber).
46. *Berceuse de Néméa* (Minkus).

47. *Souvenir : Robin des bois.*
48. *Fleur de lotus* (L'Africaine).
49. *Mazurka.*

The following additions are taken from programmes of concerts given by Saint-Léon.

50. *Le Souvenir,* fantaisie (1840).
51. *La Guaracha de Valencia, pas de deux, Allgemeiner galop* (composés pour le ballet, *Die Macht der Kunst*) (1841).
52. *L'Insensé,* concert fantast-romantique (1841).
53. Caprice sur le chanson du charpentier de *La Vita d'un giocatore* de Raimondi (1841).
54. *Il Carnevale di Venezia,* variations burlesques imités de Paganini (1842). Op. 13.
55. Grande fantaisie sur des thèmes d'*Elisa da Fosco* de Donizetti (1842).
56. *Francesca,* valse brillante (1844). Op. 16.
57. Grande fantaisie sur des thèmes d'*Eustorgia* (1844).
58. Souvenir de *Beatrice di Tenda* (1844).
59. Fantasia con reminiscenze della *Sonnambula* (1845).
60. *La Paix des champs,* duo burlesque pour chant, dialogue et violon (1850).
61. *El Carnaval Madrileño,* pour violon et violoncello (1851).
62. Fantaisie sur **Скажите ей**, chanson tzigane (1861).
63. *Sans Espoir* (1843).
64. *La Montagnarde* (1843).

Scores of the following works are to be found in the Fond Saint-Léon, Bibliothèque de l'Opéra, Paris.

Compositions for the violin

65. *Sons alpestres.* Op. 41.
66. *Vögelein im Baume* (Le Chantre des bois), idylle (1863).
67. *Rayons de bonheur,* mélodie élégiaque (1854) Op. 29

For viole d'amour

68. *Ronde pastorale,* composée pour le ballet de *Stradella* (1856) Op. 36

151

69. *Nema mia*, chanson espagnol.
70. *Mensonge du coeur*, romance, words by Alfred de Courtois.
71. *Ma Photographie*, romance, words by Poitevin (1861–62).
72. *Le Yamtschik*, chanson, words by Poitevin.

The following may also be by Arthur Saint-Léon:

L'Ange aimé, romance, words by Charles Goyneau (published in the *Musical World*, 1846, supplement, p. 85).

Provenance of the Letters

Archives Nationales, Paris, Series AJ[13] : Box 195 – Nos. 10 to 12, 45 ; Box 477 – Nos. 4 to 7 ; Box 486 – Nos. 20, 22, 27, 61, 63 ; Box 499 – Nos. 30, 34, 37 to 44, 46, 48 to 55, 57 to 60, 62 ; Box 1003A – Nos. 29, 31 to 33.

Central State Historical Archives, Moscow, Fund 497, Schedule 97 : File 16581 – No. 19 ; File 18937 – No. 21 ; File 19424 – Nos. 23 to 26, 28 ; File 20457 – Nos. 35, 36, 47 ; File 21658 – No. 56 ; File 21783 – No. 64.

Harvard Theatre Collection : Nos. 1, 13, 18.
Museum and Library of the Performing Arts, New York : No. 8.
Derra de Moroda Archives, University of Salzburg : Nos. 3, 14 to 17.
Collection of the late Mlle. Carlotta Zambelli : No. 9.
Collection of Ivor Guest : No. 2.

INDEX

154